POLITICAL INTELLIGENCE
IN
CLASSICAL GREECE

MNEMOSYNE

BIBLIOTHECA CLASSICA BATAVA

COLLEGERUNT

W. DEN BOER · W. J. VERDENIUS · R. E. H. WESTENDORP BOERMA

BIBLIOTHECAE FASCICULOS EDENDOS CURAVIT

W. J. VERDENIUS, HOMERUSLAAN 53, ZEIST

SUPPLEMENTUM TRICESIMUM PRIMUM

CHESTER G. STARR

POLITICAL INTELLIGENCE

IN

CLASSICAL GREECE

LUGDUNI BATAVORUM E. J. BRILL MCMLXXIV

POLITICAL INTELLIGENCE
IN
CLASSICAL GREECE

BY

CHESTER G. STARR

Bentley Professor of History
University of Michigan

LUGDUNI BATAVORUM E. J. BRILL MCMLXXIV

ISBN   90 04 03830 2

CONTENTS

PREFACE

The discussion which is presented in the following pages is not long, but in truth the evidence for political intelligence in Greece is not overabundant. In such a situation one might spin out hypotheses and also pile up a great abundance of modern references to the events mentioned in the text. I have, however, restricted my scope to the search for political intelligence which was connected with those events, and shall seek to marshal and to interpret the available information thereon.

Brevity does not in itself connote unimportance. The subject discussed here is a vital part of ancient interstate relations, even though it appears never to have been considered in its own right. This latter fact leads me to omit a bibliography; the more relevant modern works are cited in the notes of the introductory chapter.

CHESTER G. STARR

Ann Arbor, Michigan
June 25, 1973

CHAPTER ONE

NATURE OF THE PROBLEM

The major powers of our age have developed mighty establish-
ments in order to discover political intelligence about their possible
enemies, and friends too. Extensive funds are expended in this
search; even more impressive are the human energies and aptitudes
which are harnessed to the work. Scientists and technicians of the
most specialized skills send up spy satellites and elaborate sensitive
devices; other men and women read every journal and newspaper
and carefully file relevant data in great memory banks.

Modern superpowers need to be able to assess swiftly the potentialities of other states within a framework of rapid technological
change. The lead time, moreover, which is required to prepare one-
self against major threats must be measured in years, as the European states opposed to Hitler discovered in the 1930's. For intelli-
gent, coherent, purposeful action in relation to other powers, either
diplomatic or military, the leaders of any state must have accurate
information as to the strengths, weaknesses, and intentions of their
neighbors.

For the purposes of the present work there is no need to dwell
upon the collection and evaluation of political intelligence in the
modern world, seductive though it may be to draw parallels and
make judgments on contemporary problems. Occasionally it will
be useful to point out contrasts between the complicated political
systems of modern times and the simpler ones of the Hellenic world;
parallels will be more easily found in the period of the Ancien
Regime, i.e., the seventeenth and eighteenth centuries.

Still, it may be observed that the important subject of political
intelligence even today has not often been subjected to cool and
careful analysis in a scholarly fashion. Among the works which do
treat the problem seriously a study by Harold L. Wilensky is
illuminating in its general dicta, which will sometimes be cited in
the following pages.[1] Most of the rest of modern literature consists of

---

[1] Harold L. Wilensky, *Organizational Intelligence: Knowledge and Policy
in Government and Industry* (New York, 1967). Also sound are Fritz Machlup,
The Production and Distribution of Knowledge in the United States (Princeton,
1962), and especially on the military side Sherman Kent, *Strategic Intelligence*

partisan or thrill-seeking treatments of such "intelligence disasters" as the Japanese attack on Pearl Harbor, the German invasion of Russia in 1941, or the more recent debacle of the Cuban invasion at the Bay of Pigs.

Perhaps, then, we should not be surprised to discover that the problems of political intelligence have been little considered in the forms in which they existed in ancient Greece. On the one hand Greek states did not need to keep an eye on the technological developments of their neighbors, for change in this respect was very limited in antiquity. Yet, on the other hand, the Aegean world was a delicately interwoven tissue of hundreds of independent political units whose fortunes and misfortunes depended on external as well as on internal factors.[1]

Across the Dark Ages and even through the seventh century B.C. the *poleis* were still not fully crystallized entities which had divided the Hellenic landscape fully among themselves.[2] Thereafter, however, each of this multiplicity of states bore ever more directly on its neighbors within a very competitive system. One guiding principle of Greek life was stated briefly by Democritus, "rule belongs by nature to the stronger."[3] Another aspect of Greek politics always to be kept in mind was summed up by Plato, "Every state is in a natural state of war with every other, not indeed proclaimed by heralds, but everlasting."[4]

For the leaders of each state it was vital to know what the other constituents of the Hellenic state system—and outsiders as well—could do, and intended to do at any critical point. Political intelli-

---

for *American World Policy* (Princeton, 1949). Roberta Wohlstetter, *Pearl Harbor: Warning and Decision* (Stanford, 1962), is a good study of one catastrophe.

[1] Victor Martin, *La Vie internationale dans la Grèce des cités (VIe-IVe s. av. J.-C.)* (Paris, 1940), p. 98, stresses this aspect: "des états aussi rapprochés étaient destinés à des contacts inévitables et constants." Yet one will find nothing on political intelligence in this solid treatise, nor in any of the standard surveys of Greek political institutions (Busolt-Swoboda, Ehrenberg, et al.). The student to my knowledge which makes any useful comments is Wolfgang Riepl, *Das Nachrichtenwesen des Altertums mit besonderer Rücksicht auf die Römer* (Leipzig, 1913), who considers especially military intelligence in his last chapter (though Riepl was scarcely a prophet in his concluding remarks that the age of war correspondents had ended).

[2] See my essay, "The Early Greek City State," *La Parola del Passato* 12 (1957), pp. 97-108.

[3] Democritus fr. 267 (Diels). The Melian debate in Thucydides and many other events in Greek history show that this was not theoretical.

[4] Plato, *Laws* 1 (626a).

gence would not in itself prevent wars, but really accurate views about the problems between states must often have permitted minor adjustments which thereby made the political structure more stable and viable.

No Greek state could assume that its friends of the moment would remain so in the next upheaval. Any survey of the relations simply of Sparta, Corinth, Athens, and Thebes alone across the two centuries from Cleomenes to Philip of Macedon will illustrate the frequent diplomatic and military reversals of alliance which took place. The instability of international relations was so obvious that Sophocles could use it as an example of the inevitability of change in human history: "The same spirit is never steadfast among friends, or betwixt city and city."[1] Or, to borrow the striking phrase of one of General de Gaulle's aides, a Greek state had to be prepared à tous azimuts.

Let us look at a few famous events in Greek history where political intelligence played an important role. First, during the intense diplomatic activity just before the outbreak of the Peloponnesian War, Corinthian envoys appeared at Sparta to protest the actions of Athens at Corcyra and Potidaea. Quite clearly, to judge from Thucydides' account, the Spartans were reluctant to take action, and so the Corinthians found it necessary above all to change the picture of Athens which the Spartans entertained. "This temper of mind [i.e., spirit of trust], though favorable to moderation, too often leaves you in ignorance of what is going on outside your own country." The Spartans, that is, had a false stereotype or accepted picture of Athens in their minds. Their own king Archidamus later admitted that "when we encounter our neighbors in the Peloponnese, their forces are like our forces, and they are all within a short march"; but, as he went on to observe, the Athenians were far off and were, to boot, seamen.[2] Why, one may ask, did the Spartans have the stereotype of Athens which the Corinthians asserted they held? How did the Corinthians know otherwise about the character and policies of Athens?

Almost a century later Demosthenes delivered before the Athenian assembly a great series of speeches, including the Philippic and

---

[1] Sophocles, *Oedipus at Colonus* 612-13; cf. Euripides, *Andromache* 733-35, where Menelaus comments on a city not far from Sparta "which aforetime was friendly but now is hostile." Aeschines, *On the Embassy* 164, gives a brief example of such changes in Athenian policy.

[2] Th. 1.68, 1.80.

Olynthiac orations, which illuminated the plans of king Philip of Macedon and the dangers to Athens lurking in these plans. How did Demosthenes know the aims which his wily opponent kept within his bosom? How could he reckon, as he did, the relative strengths of the two sides by land and by sea?

An illustration of a different range of problems is afforded by Demaratus, sometime king of Sparta who was forced into exile. Like many prominent Greek fugitives he made his way to the court of the Persian king of kings, who was master of almost all the known world. Eventually Xerxes attacked Greece, and Demaratus accompanied the Persian host as an adviser on Greek, especially Spartan, political and military customs. How did the Persian king, in the first place, know that this man actually had been a Spartan king and was not an imposter? How could he judge whether the information and opinions provided by Demaratus were valid and useful? What kinds of intelligence could he gain from Demaratus?

The questions which have just been raised in three different examples have never, as far as I know, been asked. All too often the ancient historians themselves simply present information as "known", to serve as a base for a specific action.[1] One can read a work such as Aristotle's *Politics* from cover to cover and find only a few references to intelligence sources, primarily internal informers.[2] In some ways the tragic and comic stage is the most useful avenue for reflection about ancient intelligence, for the development of a plot required that the characters and also the audience be given essential information. Usually this material is provided by nurses, heralds, messengers, and the major characters themselves; but on occasion a specific twist of the drama will prove useful for our purposes.

The aim of the present work is above all to suggest that problems of political intelligence really did exist in ancient Greece; this is not an issue which is anachronistically smuggled back from modern times

---

[1] Some examples of general transmission of intelligence may be cited almost at random from the three major surviving historians of the fifth and fourth centuries: Hdt. 1.46, 1.56, 7.25; Th. 1.56, 1.57, 2.101, 4.40, 4.42, 4.108, 5.4, 5.29, 7.25, 7.32, 7.36, 8.15, 8.23, 8.63; Xen. *Hell.* 3.2, 3.4, 3.5, 4.2, 4.8, 5.2, 6.2.

[2] See p. 12, n. 2. Even foreign affairs, though considered important, are only sketchily introduced in the *Politics* (e.g., 2.3.4 [1265a. 20 ff.], 2.4.9 [1267a. 17 ff.], 4.3.13 [1291a. 19-21], 7.5.2 [1326b. 39 ff.], 7.10.2 [1330b. 1 ff.]). In the *Ethics* (Book VIII) he comments briefly on "calculations of expediency" in international relations.

even though it is true that in that simplicity the problems sometimes presented themselves in a different light. Yet the *poleis*
were not isolated entities.

If we omit technological and other aspects peculiar to the modern
world, it is proper to say that information about the potentialities
and intentions of one's neighbors was fully as important in Hellas
as today and also that this information did not necessarily lie on the
surface. In a well-known passage Polybius compares the treachery
and deceit of Philip V with the openness of "ancient" days, when
states neither used secret weapons nor sought to mislead their foes
about time and place of battle.[1] The antithesis is suspicious in
itself in view of Polybius' prejudice against Philip; insofar as it has
any validity at all it must apply to the seventh and sixth centuries
B.C. The evidence in the following pages will show that it does not
hold for the period we shall be considering.

It is easy to assert a need for intelligence. To demonstrate by
tangible examples that the need was met and to illuminate the ways
of gaining information is not so simple. One must look carefully for
almost casual hints, and at various important conjunctions the
historian can only hypothesize how the "known" information came
to be known and how it was assessed. Students of ancient Greece,
to be sure, often encounter the problem of scanty evidence; in the
present discussion it must not restrict our efforts to understand an
important aspect of international relations among the Greek states.

The period which will be considered runs from about 500 B.C. to the
accession of Alexander in 336. Before the later sixth century historical
evidence is limited and episodic, though the Homeric epics pre-
figure some of the problems and modes of intelligence which recur in
the classical era; from Alexander onwards the stage of Greek
history grows much broader and changes in character. Inevitably
Athens must play a major part in the discussion, in view of its
dominant place in classical Greek literature, but the evidence
fortunately allows us to look further in many areas.

The first aspect of the subject, considered in Chapters II and III,
will be an exploration of the methods by which information could
be gathered. This investigation must be somewhat detailed, even

---

[1] Polybius 13.3.2 ff. So one today might think back to the stylized, slow
patterns of warfare in the 18th century; cf. Emmerich de Vattel, *The Law of
Nations* (Washington, 1916, published 1758), pp. 257, 283, 304-305; J. U. Nef,
War and Human Progress (Cambridge, Mass., 1950), Part II.

though a full catalogue of ancient spies, traitors, and diplomats will not be attempted. Still, it will be useful to have a wide variety of examples inasmuch as these issues have not often been treated; occasionally much later writers will provide a particularly apt illustration.[1] Thereafter, in Chapters IV and V, the discussion will broaden out to consider the handling of intelligence within the *polis* and its limits and misuse in ancient times.

Two limits to this study should be noted at the outset. First and foremost, I shall not seek to present the historical background of events which are cited; otherwise the present work would necessarily become a general history of Greece. It is natural that the evidence is better for major crises of Greek development, such as the Persian invasion of 480-79, the Peloponnesian War of 431-04, the tangled web of interstate relations during the Spartan hegemony of 404-371, and finally the rise of Philip of Macedon after 359.

For some of these crises we have the historical works of Herodotus, Thucydides, and Xenophon; from the late fifth century onward there is an increasing volume of oratorical materials, which throw fitful lights on the handling of intelligence in the assembly. But other events could give rise to relevant information for the present theme, which may be preserved in scattered references or in the biographies of Plutarch and the collections of military stratagems made by Polyaenus and Frontinus. These three authors, who lived in the second century after Christ, were capable of making serious mistakes; still, they had access to the wide range of ancient literature which has since disappeared.

Secondly, it may be desirable to point out that the focus of attention will be political intelligence, not propaganda, though successful exploitation of propaganda themes does inevitably depend upon accurate intelligence about the enemy's ideological and physical weaknesses.[2]

To sum up the results at the outset, we shall find that the Greeks

---

[1] Translations, where offered, are normally from standard works, especially the Loeb series; in some cases they are my own. Citation of modern studies, however, must be severely restricted to the most relevant materials in view of the bulk of scholarly investigation of Greek history. It should perhaps be noted that I cannot share the belief of some recent historians that Diodorus Siculus deserves serious credit on his own; as a result he will be cited only rarely.

[2] I have tried to show the shifting lines of propaganda on one subject in "Why Did the Greeks Defeat the Persians?", *La Parola del Passato* 17 (1962), pp. 321-32.

made use at one time or another of virtually every mode of intelligence which was available in their relatively unsophisticated system of communications and technical skills.[1] These methods essentially met the purpose of providing a state with information about its neighbors, but as students of recent history know all too well, leaders do not always properly evaluate or use their available political intelligence. This failure occurred in the Greek world too at several important points, as will be noted in the conclusion of the work.

---

[1] As Riepl, *Nachrichtenwesen*, pp. 466 ff., points out, major changes in these respects came only in the nineteenth century.

CHAPTER TWO

SPIES, DESERTERS, AND TRAITORS

In modern intelligence machines the modes of acquiring information may be grouped under five general headings. First comes the intentional search by special agents and scientific tools, together with the field reports of one's own military and diplomatic personnel.[1] Secondly, other states deliberately provide information for the outside world, either publicly or surreptitiously, by means of envoys, or press and other releases. But then too the leaders of states must keep their own citizens or subjects informed if they are to gain the necessary support to carry out their plans; here again communications media, articles in journals, public speeches by leaders and their assistants, and even such long-range pronouncements as Hitler's *Mein Kampf* will be used. A fourth vehicle for information consists of commercial and industrial links. The fifth is formed by personal ties between inhabitants of different states. Nowadays these connections are likely to be in intellectual circles, but during earlier centuries of modern European history the aristocracies of many areas were bound together by ties of friendship, sport, common education, and intermarriage.

Among these modes covert methods certainly receive the greatest attention in modern literature, partly because many readers delight in tales of such great spymasters as Fouché or Gehlen, their agents (genuine or fictitious), and the wiles of M6 or the CIA. These activities, moreover, are generally linked with wartime situations, even though secret agents operate at all times, and thus borrow the glamor or infamy of the great events with which they are associated. So too the ancient evidence is fullest on the subject of spies, deserters, and traitors especially in wartime.

The procedures of military intelligence, however, are but a specialized example of more general methods of discovering the capabilities and intentions of other states. If we consider here at some length the relatively abundant information in this area for

---

[1] Here one may think in modern terms of works such as the Pentagon Papers, relating to American involvement in South Vietnam, or the many volumes of *Die grosse Politik* on interstate relations before World War I. As noted in the introductory chapter, I shall not seek to give modern parallels in a consecutive fashion throughout the present work.

Greek times, this will not be an unnecessary detour; rather, we may hope thus to determine some of the limits and possibilities of intelligence in the period. In particular, light can be thrown on the problems of evaluating information and also of preventing its leakage in the first place.

When Greek armies began to march, the most obvious method of discovering the movements and dispositions of an enemy was by the use of pickets or scouts, whose reports could be brought back by special messengers.[1] Even in this simple situation there could be difficulties. Aeneas Tacticus, who wrote a work on the defense of cities in the fourth century B.C., solemnly laid down the rule that a general must have at least three scouts at each place, men skilled in warfare so that they did not ignorantly form an opinion and alarm a city by inaccurate reports. Xenophon provides an illustration in the form of a leader of a scout party "whose judgment might be depended upon to verify the truth of the matter, with a happy gift to distinguish between fact and fiction."[2] In Euripides' *Heraclidae* Demophon, king of Athens, sends out scouts lest the Argive host catch him unawares, but then the dramatist casually has Demophon go forward himself; "for the man who thinks he knows good generalship must see the foe not by messengers alone."[3]

The reports of scouts, in other words, demanded evaluation before they were useful; and in any case the information which they could gain about an enemy's intention was necessarily limited to visual observation at a distance. To ferret more deeply, a commander could question captives, as the Greeks did at Artemisium in 480; the successful retreat of the Ten Thousand from Mesopotamia across the mountains of Armenia would scarcely have been possible had not the Greeks continually taken natives prisoner by intent or accident to serve as guides.[4] Sometimes, too, armies lay close to each

---

[1] Polyaenus 5.26 (σκοποί and δρομοκήρυκες). The messenger of Xen. *Anab.* 1.2.21 may be an example.

[2] Aeneas Tacticus 6.1; Xen. *Anab.* 4.4.15. Polyaenus 5.33.6 gives an example of the use as scouts of men who did not know each other and so would be less likely to provide false reports. There was also a difficulty in securing men who would dare to sunder themselves from the main body of troops; this was a problem also in 18th-century armies (cf. R. R. Palmer, in E. M. Earle, *Makers of Modern Strategy* [Princeton, 1943], p. 51).

[3] Euripides, *Heracleidae* 390-92.

[4] Hdt. 7.195; Xen. *Anab.* 3.5.14, 4.1.22, 4.4.16, 4.6.16, and elsewhere. Roman examples are given by Frontinus 1.2.5 (Cato in Spain; Plutarch, *Cato* 13, tells the same story with relation to Thermopylae), 1.8.9 (Caesar).

other for some time before a battle and despatched embassies to and
fro, or the soldiers themselves (as always in wartime) would frater-
nize in getting water or hunting provisions.[1]

Very often, however, the use of spies is attested, against both
external enemies and the threat of internal subversion. A detailed
list of Greek spies would begin with the wily Odysseus, who clothed
himself as a beggar and made his way safely into and out of Troy
early in the siege;[2] later, according to Sophocles' *Philoctetes*, Odysseus kept in touch with Neoptolemus on Lemnos by means of a spy
posing as a merchant. The first example too of an unmasked spy
comes from the Trojan war. The bold but unfortunate Dolon caught
by Odysseus and Ajax, was forced to reveal the Trojan dispositions
before he was killed.[3]

In historical times the spies of whom we hear are almost as often
unsuccessful as successful. Within a small *polis* the local differentia-
tions of dialect and customs caused a stranger to stand out as much
as he does in a modern Greek village, and even in major harbors
such as Rhodes and the Piraeus foreigners were probably easily
marked off if they strayed far from wharves and warehouses. Twice
in his speech "On the Crown" Demosthenes alleges the discovery of
spies at Athens, even though at least one was in hiding in the
Piraeus.[4]

Spies had better room to maneuver when they sought to penetrate
armies, especially if the enemy force were made up of mercenaries or
large, mixed contingents. Yet here too the "rascal thieves, the sort
that crawl and vex an army in the dark," were occasionally
detected.[5] The Greek spies despatched to survey Xerxes' army at
Sardis were caught, but the Persian king in his pride allowed them to
see all his mighty host and then sent them back.[6] In the next
century the Athenian general Chares, leading a mercenary force,

---

[1] Plutarch, *Timoleon* 20; Polyaenus 4.6.19. Xen. *Anab.* 3.3.5. illustrates
the desertions which could occur in these circumstances.

[2] *Odyssey* 4.242 ff.; Euripides, *Rhesus* 499 ff., 710 ff.; *Hecuba* 239.

[3] *Iliad* 10.314 ff.; Euripides, *Rhesus* passim.

[4] Demosthenes 18. 132, 137.

[5] Euripides, *Rhesus* 678. In *The Double-Cross System* (London, 1971), an
interesting report on British counter-espionage activities in World War II
which has recently been released, J. C. Masterson shows how virtually every
enemy agent was picked up, and often turned against his employer.

[6] Hdt. 7.146-47. Later repetitions of this deliberate magnanimity, by
Romans, are listed in Polyaenus 8.16.8 (cf. Livy 30.29; Appian, *Pun.* 39);
Frontinus 4.7.7 (cf. Eutropius 2.11; Zonaras 8.3); Onasander 10.9.

suspected that there were spies in his camp and had each man prove
to his companions who he was and to what unit he belonged. The
result was the capture of the enemy agents.[1] At other times,
however, spies succeeded in gaining passwords, enemy intentions,
and the strengths of opposing forces.

In the internal history of the Greek *poleis* there was, unfortunately, all too often a place for counter-intelligence, or the employment
of spies and informers. We shall come to traitors in a moment; but
to quote a general governing principle, "The more an organization
depends on the unity and support of persons, groups, factions, or
parties within its membership for the achievement of its central
goals, the more resources it will devote to the intelligence function."[2]

Among the Greek states Sparta stood in a particularly vulnerable
position, thanks to its large helot population, and maintained a
standing watch over its serfs, the famous *krypteia*. Occasionally
disaffected helots did manage to revolt, though usually only when
a natural disaster like the earthquake of 464 or outside support
encouraged insurrection; but there is evidence too for a number of
plots which were revealed to the authorities in time for their
suppression.[3] Actually, however, the main body of evidence for
counter-intelligence comes from Athens where the famous "syco-
phants" (private accusers and also informers) were well-known by the
sixth century. The *cause célèbre* which shows them best at work was
the mutilation of the Hermae in 415, after which rewards were
offered for information. Metics and slaves first came forward to
provide the initial stimulus for a great witchhunt, but eventually
even such leading citizens as Andocides sought to save their skins
by informing on others.[4] As Thucydides grimly observes, the word
of informers on this occasion was accepted without any investigation
of their reliability. A third example of internal spying is provided by

---

[1] Polyaenus 3.13.1 (cf. 5.28.2); for precautions against spies see his
discussion 5.33.1.

[2] Wilensky, *Organizational Intelligence*, p. 13.

[3] Denunciation of Pausanias by helots, Th. 1.131-32; watch after Athenian
occupation of Cythera, Th. 4.55; revelation of plot to Agesilaus, Plutarch,
Agesilaus 32.6; conspiracy of Cinadon, Xen. *Hell.* 3.3; the *krypteia*, Plutarch,
Lycurgus 28.

[4] Th. 6.27-28, 53; Plutarch, *Alcibiades* 19-21; Andocides, *On the Mysteries*
1 ff. Aristophanes' plays have frequent references to informers: *Acharnians*
819 ff.; *Knights* 437; *Peace* 191, 653; *Birds* 1410 ff.; *Ecclesiazusae* 439;
Plutus 850. Later references may be found s.v. Συκοφάντες in PW (Latte); see
especially Aristotle, *Politics* 5.4.1. (1304b. 20 ff.).

those cases where Greek political life produced tyrants or very
oligarchic structures. The concomitant often was "tale-bearers" or
participants in a plot who revealed its existence to the authorities;[1]
ladies of pleasure even had their uses in this area.[2]

Not only local political cliques could make use of their own
citizens as secret informers, but also outsiders might well hope to
gain intelligence from discontented members of an enemy state.
Modern eulogies of the communal loyalty which bound together the
citizens of a *polis* too often lead scholars to minimize the bitter
divisions which existed in Greek political practice, though one
student has recently explored in depth the activities of "fifth
columns" in the Peloponnesian War.[3] An astute outsider like king
Philip could always hope to exploit this factionalism in itself to
weaken the opposition of states such as Athens in the time of
Demosthenes;[4] but forced or voluntary exiles also had great utility
to other powers.

Deserters, traitors, and exiles, after all, were likely to know far
more about the capabilities and intentions of a *polis* than any spy
could ferret out in his hasty, surreptitious explorations. In an era,
moreover, which lacked gunpowder success in sieges depended
either on starving the defenders or securing the aid of traitors. To
judge from the relative frequency of mention in our sources, fugitives
of one sort or another were a major source of political and military
intelligence, and traitors were often of assistance in taking a town.

As the much later military writer Onasander observed, "There is
no army in which both slaves and freemen do not desert to the other
side on the many occasions that war necessarily affords," in the
hope of gaining honors and rewards.[5] Even more useful than such

---

[1] Plutarch, *Dion* 28.1, 54.3; *Pelopidas* 9; Hdt. 1.100 (Deioces); Sophocles,
Antigone 690-92, on the role of Haemon, who can hear "murmurs in the
dark."

[2] Aristotle, *Politics* 5.9.3 (1313b. 13); see also 5.9.6 (1313b. 34-5) on favors
by tyrants to women and slaves. Plutarch, *Alexander* 48.4-5 provides another
example; Riepl, *Nachrichtenwesen*, pp. 454-56, gives Roman illustrations.
Plutarch, *Pericles* 24.2 (Athenaeus 13.608-09), notes the successes of the
famous Thargelia on Persian behalf.

[3] Luis A. Losada, *The Fifth Column in the Peloponnesian War* (*Mnemosyne*,
Supplement 21, 1972). See also A. H. Chroust, "Treason and Patriotism in
Ancient Greece", *Journal of the History of Ideas* 15 (1954), pp. 280-88.

[4] E.g., Demosthenes 10.4, 18.19, 18.61, 18.295, 19.259 ff.; Polyaenus 4.2.19.

[5] Onasander 10.24. A sampling of deserters: Th. 2.57; Plutarch, *Aristides*
16.5; Hdt. 8.8, 8.82; Polyaenus 1.48.5, 2.3.10; Xen. *Anab.* 1.7.2, 2.2.7. A
citizen deserter: Lycurgus, *Against Leocrates* 17.

simple deserters were traitors and exiles who might often have held high positions in their native states before falling at odds with the dominant factions.[1] Either by outright flight or by secret messages they could provide information to an enemy.[2]

Any reader familiar with Greek history will be able to summon up quickly a variety of famous examples of deserters, traitors, and exiles. The Athenian tyrant Hippias, the Spartan king Demaratus, Themistocles himself, and many others wound up as Persian pensioners. Alcibiades avoided the threat of condemnation at Athens for the mutilation of the Hermae and profanation of the Eleusinian mysteries—as charged by informers—by fleeing to Sparta.

The list could be extended indefinitely: "There are foes without; there are traitors within," tersely comments Demosthenes.[3] More important for the present investigation are several general problems which underlie the activities and revelations of such men. First, how did deserters and other fugitives gain their information? Secondly, how reliable were their reports? And finally, how could a state hope to prevent this sort of leakage?

With respect to leaders such as Themistocles and Alcibiades, conversant with the innermost strengths and aims of their native states over a long period, the matter of knowledge is a simple one. For common citizens and ordinary soldiers, however, the source of information, apart from usual camp rumors, seems again and again to have been an assembly in which political leaders or generals informed their followers. Onasander, quoted earlier about the inevitability of deserters, prefaced this comment with the terse advice, "Thoughtless and futile is he who communicates his plan to the rank and file before it is necessary."[4]

When the Athenian generals Nicias and Demosthenes were planning to abandon the siege of Syracuse, they dared not even "by a public vote given in a numerous assembly to let their intentions

---

[1] The ubiquity of traitors may deserve a wide sample of citations: Hdt. 8.128, 9.45; Th. 1.107, 4.66, 4.76, 4.89, 4.103, 5.64, 8.44, 8.50 ff.; Xen. *Hell.* 4.4, 4.5, 6.5; Plato, *Republic* 3 (417A-B); Plutarch, *Cimon* 6.2, *Aristides* 13, *Alcibiades* 30.2, 31.2; Xen. *Anab.* 1.6.

[2] Aeneas Tacticus 31 and Frontinus 3.13 give a variety of means of sending secret messages. Cf. Hdt. 6.4; Th. 1.128-29; Plutarch, *Alcibiades* 25; Polyaenus 2.20; Xen. *Anab.* 1.6.3.

[3] Demosthenes 19.299.

[4] Onasander 10.24.

reach the enemy's ears," and on other occasions there were refusals to convene assemblies.[1] At times assemblies, though, could be used to mislead the enemy by suggesting false intentions. Aeneas Tacticus thus advised his readers to explain in an assembly of citizens or soldiers a purported night operation; for "when this is reported to the camp of the enemy, or to their city, you can divert them from what they are attempting to do."[2] The general Iphicrates prevented a Theban surprise attack on Athens by convoking his fellow citizens by night in the agora and reporting *he* had a party in Thebes ready to betray that city, so the Athenians were to march out quietly and take it. This news was promptly reported to Thebes by its agents in Athens and led the Thebans to protect themselves instead.[3] This role of assemblies in publishing political intelligence is an important matter to which we must return later.

Anyone who received covert intelligence faced very serious problems in evaluating the degree to which he could trust it. What, for instance, would the generals of Athens, encamped in 490 in the hills above Marathon, do when Ionians in the Persian force crept over at night and told the Athenian pickets that the Persian cavalry was "away"?[4] When a man rode up at night to the Greek forces at Plataea in 479, summoned the generals, stated that he was king Alexander of Macedon, and gave information that Mardonius and the Persian army would fight the next day, how did the Greek leaders know that he was whom he claimed to be or that his information was reliable?[5] If a citizen of Catana came to Syracuse in 414 and revealed the plans of the Athenian invasionary forces, how should the Syracusan generals react?[6]

This issue, how far to trust men from the other side, was always an intricate puzzle. In the first place, the deserter or traitor might be giving a true report of what he had heard, but the opposing general or political leader could have been engaged in trickery. An example of Iphicrates' cunning was noted earlier. On another occasion

---

[1] Th. 7.48, 50-51.

[2] Aeneas Tacticus 9.1-2.

[3] Polyaenus 3.9.20.

[4] Suda s.v. Χωρὶς ἱππεῖς The latest, but not very satisfactory, treatment of this passage is by N. G. L. Hammond, *Journal of Hellenic Studies* 88 (1968), pp. 39-40.

[5] Hdt. 9.45; Plutarch, *Aristides* 15.

[6] Th. 6.64; Plutarch, *Nicias* 16; Polyaenus 1.40.5. Frontinus 3.6.6 has the report given to the Syracusan assembly.

Alcibiades, besieging Byzantium, spread the report he was called off
to Ionia, ostentatiously sailed away in daylight, but returned at
night to surprise and take the city.[1] Polyaenus and other writers on
warfare give a variety of such stratagems;[2] Brasidas, the supple
Spartan commander in Macedon in the last stages of the Archidamian
war, told his troops, "The greatest reputation is gained by those stratagems in which a man deceives his enemies most completely, and
does his friends most service."[3]

In the second place, fugitives of any sort are psychologically
disturbed by the very fact of their desertion or treachery. They are
likely to tell interrogators what they feel the other side would like
to hear; and especially if they are exiles their picture may well be
unduly distorted and prejuiced. This is not the place to analyze
the Herodotean speeches which the exiled king Demaratus gave
to Xerxes, but one may note how skillfully—but probably inaccu-
rately—Herodotus made Demaratus both denigrate and praise the
qualities of the Greeks, especially the Spartans. Not to be overlooked,
moreover, is the fact that exiles rapidly lost intimate knowledge of
the policies and leaders of their former homes; how much could
Themistocles have told the Persian king about Athenian politics
even five years after the beginning of his exile?

Finally, any seasoned leader had to reckon with the possibility
that the informer he faced was deliberately lying.[4] It would be
fascinating to know how the pedagogue of Themistocles' children,
Sicinnus, made his way from the Persian guards to the presence of
Xerxes and there convinced the Persian king that the Greeks at
Salamis were really quarreling and ready to split apart—and
thereafter made his escape so that he could actually come again
with news that the Hellespontine bridge would not be destroyed.[5]

---

[1] Plutarch, *Alcibiades* 31.2-3.
[2] See also Xen. *Hell.* 3.4 (Plutarch, *Agesilaus* 10.1-2). I can only cite A. Ar-
naud, "Quelques aspects des rapports de la ruse et de la guerre dans le monde
grec du VIIIe au Ve siècle," thesis at the Sorbonne, 1971, by title.
[3] Th. 5.9.
[4] False reports by purported deserters and others are given in Hdt.
3.153 ff.; Xen. *Hell.* 5.1; and especially by Polyaenus 1.9, 1.15, 1.20, 1.42.1,
1.43.2, 2.2.4, 4.2.20, 4.6.18, 4.18.2, 5.10.3, 5.17.1, 5.33.4, 5.44.2, 6.14.5, 7.11.8,
7.12.1, 7.18.2, 7.26, 8.6; Frontinus provides others for Roman times as well as
for Greek.
[5] Perhaps for this reason Plutarch, *Themistocles* 12.3, makes Sicinnus of
Persian stock. So too the second message is delivered by a captive Persian
eunuch according to Plutarch, *Themistocles* 16.4 and *Aristides* 9.4; Polyaenus

For common deserters rules could be made, such as binding them
so that if they proved truthful they would be rewarded and, if not,
killed at once;[1] more noble traitors could perhaps be given honor-
able but firm guard; but often a leader could assess the intelligence
given to him only on the grounds of its inherent probability or
coherence with other information. In the three examples cited at the
beginning of this particular discussion, Miltiades persuaded his
fellow generals to act the very next morning on the report of the
Ionians, and so won the battle of Marathon; Pausanias and the
other Greek leaders accepted the information of king Alexander
and rearranged their forces accordingly; but in the third case, that of
the informer from Catana, the Syracusan leaders were misled by the
deception into marching on Catana so the Athenians could enter the
Great Harbor of Syracuse without opposition. Later the fatal failure
of Nicias to give up the siege of Syracuse seems to have been partly
caused by his vain hope of internal treachery.[2]

One final aspect of covert intelligence remains—how could a
state prevent its transmission to an outside power? The most
fundamental solution was not to hold assemblies and communicate
plans openly. At the beginning of the Athenian attack on Sicily
Hermocrates persuaded his fellow Syracusans to elect only three
generals who could operate secretly. At a crucial point on the march
of the Ten Thousand the Greeks temporarily decided to appoint
only one general—"If secrecy were desirable, it would be easier to
keep matters dark."[3] Alternatively, one could turn citizen against
citizen so that any possible informers were themselves informed
upon. A great part of Aeneas Tacticus' work was thus designed to
forestall internal treachery; one device was to heap up a mound of
money in the agora or an altar or temple and promise it to anyone
pointing out a conspirator.[4] In the decree by which Athens re-

---

1.30.4. There is no hint of this in Hdt. 8.75 and 8.110 (or Frontinus 2.2.14 and
2.6.8); Aeschylus, *Persians* 355 ff., calls Sicinnus ἀνὴρ γὰρ ''Ελλην. The name
turns up on Athenian vases; cf. Sikinos (3) in PW (Leonard).

[1] Onasander 10.15. Xen. *Anab.* 4.6.1 and elsewhere gives specific illustrations.

[2] Th. 7.48, 73 (Plutarch, *Nicias* 18, 21, 26); Polyaenus 1.43.2; Frontinus
2.9.7; cf. Peter Green, *Armada from Athens*, (New York, 1970), pp. 5, 205 ff.,
291 ff.

[3] Th. 6.72-3; Xen. *Anab.* 6.1.18. Cf. Th. 8.7 and 8.9 on other examples of
secrecy; Hdt. 6.132 on Miltiades' expedition; and on sealed letters to subordi-
nates Polyaenus 4.7.2 and Frontinus 1.1.2.

[4] Aeneas Tacticus 10.15.

arranged the government of Chalcis after its revolt (445 B.C.), the oath laid upon the Chalcidians required them to reveal anyone planning a revolt.[1]

Again, authorities could prevent the access of untrustworthy persons to arsenals and dockyards. The one case in which we are specifically informed that such sensitive areas were guarded comes from the Hellenistic age, when Rhodes protected its dockyards;[2] but very probably any prying person found around the Athenian naval base on the east side of the Piraeus promontory would soon have had to explain his presence. Demosthenes, the ever vigilant watchman for Athenian democracy, even indicates that he had caught in hiding a man who had promised Philip of Macedon to burn the dockyards.[3]

The last step which could be taken was censorship proper. Aeneas Tacticus ordered that no one should receive letters from exiles or send them; "outgoing and incoming letters shall be brought to censors before being sent out or delivered."[4] All towns shut their gates at night by elaborate procedures to make certain that even the guards could not open them, and by day as well some controls were exercised, both at the gates and occasionally on the roads. Persian censorship on the great roads of the empire was famous, and seems to have been thorough enough that Histiaeus had to resort to the device of tattooing a message on the head of a slave and then allowing his hair to grow again before sending him down the Royal Road to Ionia.[5] At least in Spartan territories we also have brief references to guards on the roads,[6] and there seems to

---

[1] H. Bengtson, *Die Staatsverträge des Altertums*, II (Munich, 1962), no. 155, lines 24-25 (= Tod, *GHI*, no. 42); for the later history of this type of oath see Peter Herrmann, *Der römische Kaisereid* (Göttingen, 1968), p. 28, n. 30.

[2] Strabo 14.2.5; the attempt by Philip's agent Heracleides is noted in Polybius 13.4-5 and Polyaenus 5.17.1.

[3] Demosthenes 18.132 (Plutarch, *Demosthenes* 14.4). Here, as so often, one would wish to know more: by what counter-intelligence means did Demosthenes discover the plot? Another piece of evidence suggesting a guard is perhaps the fragmentary comment of Hyperides, *In Defense of Lycophron* 1, frag. IIIa, "the betrayal of dockyards."

[4] Aeneas Tacticus 10.6. A number of the messages listed above p. 13 n. 2 (as Xen. *Anab.* 1.6.3) were intercepted.

[5] Hdt. 5.35, cf. 1.123, 5.52; Riepl, *Nachrichtenwesen*, pp. 282 ff. Interesting light on Persian authorizations for travel is thrown by the travel rations itemized in R. T. Hallock, *Persepolis Fortification Tablets* (Oriental Institute Publications 92, Chicago, 1969), nos. PF 1285-1579, 2049-57.

[6] Polyaenus 3.9.57. In Euripides, *Iphigenia at Aulis* 303 ff. Menelaus somewhat accidentally acts as a road-guard.

have been some use of passports or permits to travel, judging from a reference in Aristophanes.[1] News could also be suppressed by public edict or by the wiles of a general.[2]

In their own eyes spies, deserters, traitors, and vengeful exiles may have been moved by the most noble patriotic or ideological motives in ancient Greece just as scientific, diplomatic, and other personnel have been in the twentieth century. Still, human societies, though excited by these exploits or treacheries, do not generally give their perpetrators the credit they ascribe to themselves. From the point of view of gaining political intelligence these reports were all subject to defects and often to distortion. Worse yet, leaders in all ages have often been prone to evaluate secret intelligence too highly. As Wilensky observes, the very accent on secrecy "impairs critical judgment in the production and interpretation of intelligence and dulls the sense of relevance."[3]

Another important comment by this student of modern political intelligence may well be put as a conclusion to a summation of the avenues of secret intelligence in Greece: "In the end, the most reliable intelligence sources for competing organizations are open; the best data, seldom secret, are the actions of the other party."[4]

---

[1] Aristophanes, *Birds* 1212-15; Aeneas Tacticus 10.8 ordains no citizen or metic shall sail without a *symbolon* (though this term usually has another significance; cf. Kahrstedt s.v. in PW).

[2] The Thebans thus voted that if anyone carried arms through Boeotia to aid the revolt against the Thirty at Athens "no Theban would either see him or hear about it" (Plutarch, *Lysander* 27.3, and *Pelopidas* 6.4; Dinarchus, *Against Demosthenes* 25). For suppression by a general see e.g., Plutarch, *Agesilaus* 17.3; Xen. *Hell.* 4.3; Polyaenus 2.1.3.

[3] Wilensky, *Organizational Intelligence*, p. 66.

[4] Wilensky, p. 72.

CHAPTER THREE

AMBASSADORS, MERCHANTS, AND ARISTOCRATS

Open sources of intelligence are more significant today than covert methods, if we may accept the general observations of Wilensky quoted at the close of the previous chapter. In the world of the *polis* the validity of this evaluation would appear to be even more evident.

Efforts at secrecy were spasmodic and not very successful. One of the most elaborate plans in this direction is recounted by Xenophon at the beginning of the *Anabasis*, but while Cyrus the Younger did keep his common soldiers in the dark for some time the satrap Tissaphernes was not misled by the outward purposes of Cyrus' preparations and reported promptly to the king.[1] Even in the modern world coherent efforts toward maintaining continuous security of important developments or information scarcely began before the nineteenth century; and as we all know have rarely been totally effective. Moreover, the decision-making body in most Greek states was an assembly of citizens. Once problems or plans had been laid before such a body, they were likely to spread abroad by a variety of avenues, both intentional and unintentional.[2]

Unfortunately there is far less evidence about open methods of intelligence-gathering, partly perhaps because they were open. Historians are wont simply to report that "the news came" or that something became "known." If they go further in illuminating the source, the usual device is to say that a messenger came.[3] In one such case Thucydides incidentally comments that the news about the attack on Plataea had already reached Athens before the messenger arrived;[4] this report is perhaps the best illustration for the

---

[1] Xen. *Anab.* 1.1 ff., esp. 1.2.4, 1.4.11-12.

[2] See the examples noted above on p. 14; this subject will recur in Chapter IV.

[3] A few messages: Th. 3.3 (one of our most detailed accounts of the mode of travel of a messenger); Hdt. 6.105 (the runner Philippides); Plutarch, *Timoleon* 18.3 and *Dion* 26 (a fascinating account of how a message might *not* be delivered); Th. 6.21 (Nicias' complaint that during the four winter months one could hardly send a message from Sicily to Athens; cf. the time-delay in the publication of edicts in the late Roman Empire). The Athenian sacred ships Paralus and Salaminia also conveyed messages (Th. 8.74, Xen. *Hell.* 2.1-2). See Riepl, *Nachrichtenwesen*, pp. 123 ff.

[4] Th. 2.6.

existence in Greece of that anonymous, almost inexplicable means of communications which is called in modern times "the bush telegraph."

Even so, some evidence does exist to permit a limited exploration of the various vehicles of open intelligence, though it is not always possible to determine their relative significance in any given situation. These modes consists of ambassadors, merchants and other travellers, and aristocrats.

The major deliberate forms of communications between states are visible with some clarity. Greek states did not have standing embassies in other communities, but there would appear to have been an almost constant procession of ambassadors to and fro on specific matters, both to other states and to the great religious shrines.[1] In the deliberations at Sparta before the outbreak of the Peloponnesian War Athenian envoys happened to be on hand for other reasons who could, as Thucydides put it, remind the elder men of what they knew and inform the younger of what lay beyond their experience.[2] In opposing Philip, Demosthenes repeatedly urged that embassies be sent "in every direction to instruct, to exhort, to act."[3]

Embassies could put forward the problems and views of their native states, but like diplomatic personnel in more recent times they could also gain valuable information about the situation in the states to which they were directed. Demosthenes in his rebuttal to Aeschines stressed the importance of ambassador's reports; "you reach a right decision if they are true, a wrong decision if they are false."[4]

In part this information was derived from open meetings with officials and, if permitted, by the appearance of the ambassadors at assemblies; but to a greater degree it was probably gained by informal communications. Aeneas Tacticus warned that ambassadors are to have no private discourse without "certain of the most trusted citizens" present;[5] Herodotus portrayed the Persian

---

[1] See generally Coleman Philippson, *The International Law and Customs of Ancient Greece and Rome*, I (London, 1912), pp. 147-56 (*proxenia*), 302-46 (embassies). D. J. Mosley, *Envoys and Diplomacy in Ancient Greece*, was announced for publication as a *Historia* Einzelschrift after the present essay was completed.

[2] Th. 1.72.

[3] Demosthenes 1.2, 8.76, 9.72, 18.79.

[4] Demosthenes 19.5.

[5] Aeneas Tacticus 10.11. Note the care in dealing with Persian envoys in Xen. *Anab.* 2.3.8, 2.3.21; and Aeschines' remarks (*Against Ctesiphon* 250) on

ambassadors of Cambyses to Ethiopia as acting virtually as spies.[1]

An important institution in this connection was the regular existence of *proxenoi*, citizens of one state appointed to (or inheriting) the responsibility of protecting the interests of citizens of another state. Ambassadors often turned to the local *proxenos* for advice as to how to present their cause, and in the famous example of Alcibiades, Spartan *proxenos* at Athens, one set of Spartan envoys was thereby tricked into making fools of themselves in the Athenian assembly.[2] In at least one other case these representatives were not to be trusted; Arthmius of Zeleia became infamous for serving as a Persian agent in the Peloponnesus even though he was *proxenos* of Athens.[3] On the whole, nonetheless, the *proxenoi* performed their duty seriously. At times a *proxenos* could even provide independent reports to the state with which he was linked.

Polydamus of Pharsalus thus made a trip to Sparta in 374 and, as reported by Xenophon, stated that "it is my duty as *proxenos* and benefactor (titles borne by my ancestry from time immemorial) that I claim, or rather am bound, in case of any difficulty to come to you, and, in case of any complication dangerous to your interests in Thessaly, to give you warning." So he proceeded to alert the Spartans to the threat presented by Jason of Pherae and summed up the numbers of men Jason would have if he united all Thessaly. Later in the same book of the *Hellenica* Xenophon cites Callias of Athens, likewise a *proxenos* of Sparta, who had been to Sparta twice to arrange a truce. In his *Anabasis* a proxenus acts not only as intermediary but also as interpreter; Thucydides refers to *proxenoi* serving as informers or intermediaries.[4]

Beyond formal embassies and the intervention of *proxenoi* international relations rested on a flow of heralds bearing messages

the tendency at the time of the speech for letters and ambassadors to be directed to private individuals rather than the council and assembly.

[1] Hdt. 3.17, 3.22-24; cf. the exploits of Democedes, Hdt. 3.134-36.

[2] Th. 5.45; Plutarch, *Alcibiades*, 14.6-9. Cf. the expectation in Aeschylus, *Suppliants* 919, that the Egyptian herald will have appealed προξένοις, and Aeschines' assertion (*Against Ctesiphon* 72) that Demosthenes had arranged beforehand with Antipater, a Macedonian envoy, as to the latter's statement to the assembly.

[3] Aeschines, *Against Ctesiphon* 258; Dinarchus, *Against Aristogeiton* 24; Demosthenes 9.42 and 19.271. See recently G. E. M. de Ste Croix, *The Origins of the Peloponnesian War* (Ithaca, N.Y., 1972), p. 189, n. 79.

[4] Xen. *Hell.* 6.1, 6.2; Xen. *Anab.* 5.4.1 ff.; Th. 3.2, 5.59; Aeschines, *On the Embassy* 172.

and decrees;[1] on the tragic stage heralds appear frequently to provide information or to issue threats, as in Euripides' *Heracleidae*. Their formal position in the Greek world stood higher than did that of *praecones* in Rome, and at times they can hardly be distinguished from ambassadors proper.

Less formal, and far less well illuminated, is the activity of merchants. To revert briefly to a critical debate mentioned at the beginning of this essay the Corinthians emphasized to the Spartans in the discussions before the opening of the Peloponnesian War that inlanders did not know the full situation; but "those among us who have ever had dealings with the Athenians, do not require to be warned against them."[2] The reference may be mainly to political contact, but a modern student will suspect that if the Corinthians were aware of Athenian intentions the evidence must have come partly through commercial relations.

From the time when the Greeks again began to trade out across the Mediterranean to Syria in the east and to Sicily and beyond in the west, merchants brought back ideas and techniques, such as the alphabet and the use of molds to make clay figurines, as well as carrying abroad the vases and other physical products which appear in archaeological contexts. Along with ideas must have come information, as we can detect in one particular aspect. Geographical relationships, that is, were already becoming clearer in the Homeric Hymns than they had been in the epics proper; by the sixth century B.C. someone seems to have set down a survey of the Spanish coast which served as a source for the much later Avienus. The *Periegesis* which Hecataeus of Miletus had written by about 510 was a detailed, systematic description of Mediterranean coasts and various inland districts.[3]

By classical times the merchants who scurried over the Aegean and farther afield in their tiny craft were numerous; Plato could only dream wistfully of an ideal state which did not have seaborne contacts. By the interplay of trade the merchants of many communities must have picked up far more than geographic and climatic information and curiosities. Undoubtedly they brought back bits of news to their home agoras, which were fed into public knowledge,

---

[1] Heralds for general information, Plutarch, *Timoleon* 23; in time of war e.g., Hdt. 1.21-22, Th. 6.50, 7.3; cf. Riepl, *Nachrichtenwesen*, p. 330.

[2] Th. 1.120.

[3] See my *Awakening of the Greek Historical Spirit* (New York, 1968), pp. 44 ff. Cf. the report by the dealer in purple from Itanus in Hdt. 4.151.

though the aristocratic bias of ancient culture gives us only a few examples of the process.

For illustrations of the general broadcasting of information by merchants one may cite first the traders dealing with the Ten Thousand, who were told that Xenophon planned to settle the soldiers on the Pontic coast and carried the news back to their cities. Or again, Lycurgus levied as a significant charge against Leocrates the fact that when he hastily abandoned Athens after the battle of Chaeronea he reported the disaster both officially and to the merchants of Rhodes, "merchants who sailed round the whole Greek world on their business and passed on the news of Athens which they had heard from Leocrates."[1] If Lysias may be believed, grain merchants in particular were capable of inventing rumors as well as getting news before anyone else.[2]

A more specific conveyance of intelligence is the story of the Syracusan Herodas, who "happened" to be in Phoenicia with a shipowner and there saw many triremes as well as hearing that 300 warships were to be made ready. Herodas thereupon took the first ship to Greece and reported the information to the Spartans, who immediately convoked their allies and began to make ready for a war with Persia.[3] Against such seaborne leakage of information Alcibiades once ordered all small trading craft seized so that Mindarus, in the Hellespont, could get no news of his approach.[4] Spies and agents also at times adopted the pose of merchants, which could justify their movements.[5]

The most famous example of commercial communication of information is in Plutarch's *Life of Nicias* and seems almost to be a story "bien trouvée." After the disastrous end of the Athenian expedition to Syracuse a stranger is reported to have landed at the Piraeus and in the barbershop casually happened to refer to the catastrophe, which was not yet known in Athens. The barber threw down his tools and ran to the city proper, where he blurted out the news to the archons and in the agora.[6] The troubles which then

---

[1] Xen. *Anab.* 5.6.21; Lycurgus, *Against Leocrates* 14-15.

[2] Lysias 22.14.

[3] Xen. *Hell.* 3.4.

[4] Xen. *Hell.* 1.1; Plutarch, *Alcibiades* 28.

[5] Plutarch, *Pelopidas* 14.2.

[6] Plutarch, *Nicias* 30. Th. 8.1. observes only that the news was brought to Athens, but the Athenians refused to believe it even though they had the word of soldiers who had escaped.

befell the barber as a rumor-monger will recur in the next chapter, in connection with the handling of intelligence.

Even more suggestive of the problems of seaborne information is a brief fragment in which Eunapius at Constantinople in the late Roman Empire speaks of the affairs of Stilicho in Italy. Though far beyond the confines of our period it deserves quotation:

> It was impossible to discover any accurate information concerning the West. Owing to the length of the voyage, news took a long time to arrive, and was distorted when it came. Travellers and soldiers with access to information about affairs of state spoke according to their own personal likes or dislikes. If you collected three or four of them together with their rival versions as witnesses, quite a quarrel would ensue, beginning with questions like 'What was your source for that?', 'Where did Stilicho see you?', 'And where could you have seen the eunuch?' So that it was a job to decide between them. Merchants told nothing but lies, or what would bring them some gain . . .[1]

This passage makes it clear that merchants were an important, if unreliable source of information; but it is interesting also for its vague mention of "travellers" as distinct from merchants. These travellers turn up also in Greek contexts; "many rumors from wayfarers are wont to go abroad."[2] When Themistocles was stalling at Sparta while his fellow citizens built a wall around their city in 479/8, travellers kept reporting to the Spartans that this construction was under way.[3] On other occasions as well they conveyed intelligence; it almost appears that the roads of Greece were always thronged with hosts of eager—and able—information-purveyors.

Who were these travellers? Sometimes they were actors, who could even be used as ambassadors by reason of the popularity of their art.[4] Others who moved about with considerable freedom were musicians, poets, and thinkers. Aeschylus went to Sicily; Euripides, to Macedonia; Pindar, to many states. Pythagoras and Xenophanes moved from Asia Minor to Italy in the sixth century; the sophists of the later fifth century were often famous for the ease

---

[1] Eunapius fr. 74 (*FHG* 4.46b), translated by Alan Cameron, *Claudian* (Oxford, 1970), p. 246. Riepl, *Nachrichtenwesen*, pp. 445-47, gives other examples of merchants in Roman history.

[2] Sophocles, *Oedipus at Colonus* 303-04.

[3] Th. 1.91.

[4] Aeschines, *On the Embassy* 15, and Demosthenes 18.21 on the actor Aristodemus; cf. his contemporary and colleague Neoptolemus, Demosthenes 5.6.

with which they shifted from one temporary abode to the next. Seekers of religious shrines were also on the roads, as were mercenaries on their way to employment; but common folk proper were probably less likely to undertake the risks of travel abroad than were aristocrats, who could rely on a network of friendships and were escorted by a retinue of servants and guards. Examples are Dion's travels in exile, probably too the wide-flung wanderings of Herodotus, or the legendary visit to Greece by Anacharsis.[1]

In these and other international activities and connections among the aristocracies of Greece we come without question to the most important threads in the web of open communications. Aristocrats could move more easily and safely than ordinary citizens, and were more accustomed to do so. When they did travel, they observed more consciously and on a more political level, for aristocrats provided the leadership in almost all Greek states.

Yet the manifold ways in which aristocrats could gain information are the most poorly illuminated aspect of our subject. In antiquity the ties among aristocrats of different states were very commonly taken for granted in a culture which was aristocratically based; modern studies of the upper classes in ancient Greece usually consider only such intellectual aspects as are discussed by Werner Jaeger in his *Paideia*. For many important political and social aspects of this governing elite serious investigation is still to come.[2]

At this point the important requirement is to suggest, if only in a general way, the many types of aristocratic links which could serve as conduits for political intelligence. The most intimate, no doubt, was international marriages of aristocrats, which seem to have taken place as often as in early modern Europe. Pindar had connections with a clan spread across Sparta, Thera, and Cyrene; a number of Athenian leaders in the sixth and fifth centuries had foreign mothers

---

[1] E.g., Plutarch, *Dion* 17.3, and *Alexander* 9.6 (Demaratus of Corinth); Hdt. 4.77 (Anacharsis); note the variety of visitors to Athens listed in Xenophon, *Ways and Means* 5. Cf. A. Heuss, *Antike und Abendland* 2 (1946), pp. 49-50, who feels (pp. 42-33) that the lower classes moved freely also.

[2] R. R. Bolgar in Robert Wilkinson, ed., *Governing Elites: Studies in Training and Selection* (New York, 1969), pp. 23-49, is not very useful; Heuss, *Antike und Abendland* 2 (1946), pp. 49-50, is brief but suggestive. One cannot indeed cite many works on modern aristocracies from this point of view; see e.g., Andrew Sinclair, *The Last of the Best: The Aristocracy of Europe in the Twentieth Century* (London, 1969).

or wives.[1] The long-protracted wooing of Agariste, daughter of Cleisthenes of Sicyon, brought nobles from all over Greece, who are duly itemized by Herodotus. On this occasion, parenthetically, the conversation and entertainment may at times have produced no more than the spectacle of Hippocleides dancing on a table, but at other points the many noble suitors must have measured each other's countries and costumes in their discourses.[2]

From the days when Achilles, Ajax, and other Homeric heroes were educated by the centaur Chiron on to the appointment of Aristotle as tutor for Alexander, education was an international bond of aristocrats. Pindar is said to have studied at Athens; Sappho drew aristocratic daughters from much of the east coast of the Aegean; the students of Plato, Isocrates, and Aristotle came from many parts of the Greek world. Normally this aspect is mentioned by modern scholars with regard to its significance in inculcating common standards of judgment and behavior; but even if the days of the Second Sophistic were yet to come movement for educational purposes could also bring transfer of information.

Beyond marriage and education, aristocrats were linked across the borders of states through the institution of guest-friendships, which were inherited, and by other ties of less formalized character. As Agesilaus put it, "within the states of Hellas the folk of one country contract relations of friendship and hospitality with one another."[3] His Athenian contemporary, Andocides, could empha-

---

[1] Pindar, *Pyth.* 5.72 ff. (and scholia); John K. Davies, *Athenian Propertied Families, 600-300 B.C.* (Oxford, 1971), provides information on Pisistratus, Themistocles, Cimon, Pericles, and others. L. Gernet, "Mariages de tyrans," in *Anthropologie de la Grèce antique* (Paris, 1968), pp. 344-58, is brief, as is his preceding essay on nobles. There is no need to cite here the Homeric evidence.

[2] Hdt. 6.126-30. Hippocleides himself was connected to the Cypselids in Corinth; for this and other Athenian external connections see G. Daverio Rocchi, *Rendiconti*, Istituto Lombardo, classe di lettere 105 (1971), pp. 553-55.

[3] Xen. *Hell.* 4.1. Agesilaus goes on to say that in time of war friend will fight friend even so; but the *Iliad*, for example, shows that ties of friendship could quickly be resumed in times of truce. I cannot forebear quoting the charming picture noted by Goldoni in Italy in 1733 at a break in a siege (quoted by Nef, *War and Human Progress*, pp. 158-59): "A bridge thrown over the breach afforded a communication between the besiegers and the besieged: tables were spread in every quarter, and the officers entertained one another by turns: within and without, under tents and arbors, there was nothing but balls, entertainments and concerts. All the people of the environs flocked there on foot, on horseback, and in carriages: provisions arrived from every quarter; abundance was seen in a moment, and there was no want of stage doctors and tumblers. It was a charming fair, a delightful rendezvous."

size the utility to Athens of his "ties and friendships with kings, with states, and with individuals too, in plenty. Acquit me, and you will share in them all, and be able to make use of them whenever occasion may arise."[1]

Along this network information could travel both by personal movement and also by messages and letters. Histaeus despatched a slave with a secret message to Aristagoras; Archias of Athens revealed, but too late, the plot of Pelopidas in a letter to his guest-friend Archias of Thebes.[2] When Lysander was in Asia, the Spartans received letters of complaint about his behavior, but apparently from people of little weight in Spartan eyes; only when the satrap Pharnabazus himself wrote did the Spartan ephors realize that the reports required action.[3]

For individual travels by aristocrats there are only scattered references, such as the trip of Solon to Egypt "for business and for sight-seeing."[4] In classic times it is probably incorrect to postulate the regular circuit of touring and visual education which the Roman aristocrats Cicero, Caesar, and others engaged in during the last century of the Republic, or the Grand Tour of English aristocrats in the 18th century;[5] and yet Greek aristocratic fathers probably did see to it that their sons gained an acquaintance with areas and nobles outside their native states. By visits to relatives or by sporting events (such as the legendary hunt of the Calydonian boar, to which Meleager invited the great nobles of Greece) personal ties could be maintained or enlarged.

The greatest gatherings of aristocrats undoubtedly occurred on the occasions of the major festivals and games of the Greek world, which gave opportunities for public political speeches by men like Gorgias and Lysias and for less formal conversations and dinners

---

[1] Andocides, *On the Mysteries* 145. In his earlier speech, *On His Return*, he cited several practical advantages of these connections.

[2] Plutarch, *Pelopidas* 10.3.

[3] Plutarch, *Lysander* 19.

[4] *Ath. Pol.* 11.1; Hdt. 1.29 views this differently. See recently G. Daverio Rocchi, *Rendiconti*, Istituto Lombardo, classe di lettere 105 (1971), pp. 534-35.

[5] On the Grand Tour in particular we may be inclined to think first of its artistic and literary side, as revealed in the travels of Boswell or Goethe; but activities included also hunting with princes and association with the nobles of other lands. See recently Geoffrey Trease, *The Grand Tour* (New York, 1967). For the connections of Roman and Greek aristocrats in the late Republic it will suffice to cite the career of Cicero and in particular his brief observations in *Epp. ad Quintum Fratrem* 1.1.5.

as well. In modern studies there is a strong tendency to view the prophetic center of Delphi in particular as a sounding-board for ancient Greece. Its temple personnel must have known a great deal about the strengths and aims of Greek states at least by the classic period, and a sceptic may surmise that this information helped to determine the interpretation of the responses given by the Pythia to state inquiries. Thus Delphic advice did have its effect in directing the specific location of colonies by the sixth century at least.[1] Even so it was the congregation of aristocrats on major occasions at Delphi and Olympia that served as the main force by which information was spread via religious centers.

The subjects discussed at such meetings could have been purely personal; they probably were political on occasion; they could also have been religious, for one can never overlook the intertwining of religion and the *polis*. Oracles, true or forged, were a powerful vehicle for political attack or an encouragement to military activity, if one state knew that another was divinely threatened for some misdeed or open to a particular weakness.[2] Again, the occasions of local religious ceremonies were seized upon more than once by an enemy for a surprise attack.[3]

The kind of knowledge required for events of this last type might have been a common possession, but to a large degree the intimate knowledge of the personalities of leaders of other states and of the direction in which their policies tended must have been stored mainly in noble memories. Specific bits of intelligence gain their full weight only when they can be placed against a wide background of information, and this fund of knowledge was provided especially by the wide network of aristocratic connections which have just been surveyed. Here, however, we approach the more general problems of the assessment, handling, and preservation of political intelligence, which deserve special consideration.

---

[1] H. W. Parke and D. E. W. Wormell, *The Delphic Oracle*, I (Oxford, 1956), pp. 49 ff. But note the cautions expressed by Jean Defradas, *Les Thèmes de la propagande delphique* (Paris, 1954), pp. 233 ff., and W. G. Forrest, "Colonisation and the Rise of Delphi," *Historia* 6 (1957), pp. 160-75.

[2] Hdt. 1.20; Demosthenes 14.25; Polyaenus 3.5; on propagation of oracles cf. Plutarch, *Nicias* 13 (*Alcibiades* 17) and *Lysander* 25. The oracle about the body of Oedipus is a basic factor in Sophocles, *Oedipus at Colonus*. M. P. Nilsson, *Cults, Myths, Oracles and Politics in Ancient Greece* (Lund, 1951), is more concerned with their propagandistic side.

[3] Aristophanes, *Acharnians* 1076-77; Th. 3.3; Plutarch, *Pelopidas* 5.3. Much later, Vespasian attacked the Jews on the Sabbath (Frontinus 2.1.17).

CHAPTER FOUR

THE HANDLING OF INTELLIGENCE

Every scrap of information, however insignificant in outward appearance, may provide grist for the mills of modern intelligence. Moreover, vital intelligence does not necessarily have to be covert; to quote Wilensky again, "a sophisticated reporter working with open sources is better than an agent working with top-secret information."

The mass, indeed, of raw information pouring into the offices of a Central Intelligence Agency is almost incredible in volume. The danger, if anything, is that the important scrap may be lost in the mound and that those responsible for handling intelligence and for presenting the results to political and military leaders will over-whelm them with meaningless quantities of statistical character, "a surfeit of information, useless, poorly integrated."[1]

Ancient life was far simpler, and the ways of gaining information which have been surveyed in the two preceding chapters undoubted-ly provided specific pieces of intelligence in a slow, almost haphazard fashion. Nonetheless the basic problems of handling, assessing, and acting on intelligence were as challenging as in modern times.

On the tragic stage information is very often, though not always, a problem. The characters may engage in self-deception or, at the outset, not know essential facts, as Jocaste, mother and wife of Oedipus. In the course of a play one person may seek to deceive others by actions or by words, as in the case of Philoctetes on Lemnos. Almost always, however, the audience itself is not deliber-ately misled—one of the most conspicuous exceptions is the speech by Lichas in Sophocles' *Trachiniae* (225 ff.)—and indeed the characters themselves are normally truly informed, not deceived, by messengers, heralds, and other agents during the development of the play.[2] They stand, in other words, on the same base of know-

---

[1] Wilensky, *Organizational Intelligence*, pp. 180, vii.

[2] As Ursula Parlavantza-Friedrich, *Täuschungsszenen in den Tragödien des Sophokles* (Berlin, 1969), p. 10, observes, the spectator "in den meisten Fällen vorher von der Wahrheit unterrichtet wird"; cf. pp. 82 ff. For Euripi-des see the essay by H. Strohm in *Würzburger Jahrbücher für die Altertums-wissenschaft* 4 (1949), pp. 140-56. (I am much indebted on this aspect to a fruitful discussion with Prof. Charles Segal.)

ledge as the audience, and all are given sufficient information to act as well as to judge. Athenian audiences did not have to cope with bewilderingly erroneous or incomplete intelligence to the degree which marks many of Shakespeare's plays or *Le Nozze di Figaro*.

In the real politics of ancient Greece, however, the evidence for foreign intentions did not necessarily develop with the essential sureness of the tragic stage. The problems which must rise in our investigation at this point are two: first, what types of information the intelligence procedures available to a Greek state could provide; and, secondly, how this intelligence was handled so as to guide public decisions.

Above all, the leaders of Athens, Thebes, and other powers must have wished to know the political intentions of their neighbors. This subject included the danger of war, the nature of alliances, internal divisions, and the characteristics of opposing leaders.[1] When Spithridates deserted from the Persians to the Spartans in 396, Agesilaus "set himself at once to get information about Pharnabazus, his territory and his government."[2]

There are also occasional indications that military capabilities, including geographical information, were the subject of deliberate investigation. As a child Alexander entertained Persian envoys sent to his father, and impressed them by his searching questions about the length of roads, the character of the journey, the military abilities of the Persian kings, and the prowess and might of the Persians.[3] In much earlier times Phanes of Halicarnassus, a mercenary in the service of king Amasis of Egypt, fled to Cambyses despite pursuit by Amasis' officers, for he "could give very exact intelligence about Egypt."[4] This information, according to Herodotus, included especially advice as to how to cross the desert between Palestine and Egypt. Perhaps the most famous traitor in Greek times was Alcibiades, who promised according to Thucydides that insofar as he had

---

[1] On the rising prominence of generals and magistrates, the outburst of Peleus in Euripides, *Andromache* 693 ff., seems to be a reflection of current events; note the effectiveness of Brasidas' reputation in Th. 4.81. As F. G. Bailey, *Stratagems and Spoils* (New York, 1969), p. 59, points out, leaders become significant only in eras in which innovation breaks ancestral patterns of reaction—the very type of eras in which intelligence becomes more important.

[2] Xen. *Hell.* 3.4.

[3] Plutarch, *Alexander* 5.1.

[4] Hdt. 3.4.

better information he was bound to instruct the Spartans on Athenian plans. Actually we do not know how fully he discoursed about Athenian affairs; but the specific pieces of advice he gave—to fortify Decelea, to drum up new war at home, and to send Gylippus to help the Syracusans—fell in the military sphere.[1]

The most precise description of the types of military information which a deserter could provide an enemy comes from the late Roman Empire, when the *protector* Antoninus, mistreated by the authorities, planned carefully his flight to the Persians. Before doing so he pried into all parts of the Empire,

> and being versed in the language of both tongues, busied himself with calculations, making record of what troops were serving anywhere or of what strength, or at what time expeditions would be made, inquiring also by tireless questioning whether supplies of arms, provisions, and other things that would be useful in war were at hand in abundance.[2]

Equipped with this information, Antoninus succeeded in making his way across the border, despite the guards, and joined the Persians.

The socio-economic structure and strength of enemies and friends are prime concerns in modern intelligence. In the Greek world changes in these matters were as a rule so slow that they probably required no special attention; yet there are interesting hints that the Greeks did not entirely neglect them. The Athenians sent ambassadors to Segesta to determine if it could provide the financial support which it promised for the Syracusan expedition; so too the greedy Polycrates of Samos had his secretary check the treasury of Oroetes.[3] Demographic interests are attested by a fascinatingly modern-sounding story which Polyaenus reports. Once upon a time Memnon, the Persian commander, sent an ambassador to Leucon, tyrant of the Crimean Bosporus; this envoy was accompanied by a famous musician, Aristonicus of Olynthus. Everywhere they landed Aristonicus performed so that the ambassador could estimate from the crowds in the theaters the population of the several cities.[4]

As will be shown in the next chapter, there were limits to the degree to which one state could establish quantitative data about the population and wealth of its neighbors, though rough figures

---

[1] Th. 6.89-92, 8.12; Plutarch, *Alcibiades* 23.2; Polyaenus 1.40.6.
[2] Ammianus Marcellinus 18.5.1.
[3] Th. 6.6, 6.8, 6.46-7; Polyaenus 6.21; Hdt. 3.123.
[4] Polyaenus 5.44.1.

could be achieved and used as one basis for decisions as to possible actions. In another type of intelligence, however, the Greek world was far more active than a modern intelligence agency would be; examples of the use of oracles and the knowledge of times of religious festivals were given earlier.

However obtained, political, military and other information had to be processed, analyzed, and if desirable published. The bearers of intelligence, including ambassadors and heralds, were expected to report first to the leading political officers of a state. In Sparta by the fifth century the ephors had taken away control of the reception and handling of information from the kings, who exercised the function earlier.[1] For Athens the *Constitution of the Athenians* gives the rule that heralds, ambassadors, and bearers of letters reported to the prytanes first; Aeschines goes on to state that ambassadors could address the assembly only if permitted by a decree of the council.[2] Even in the moving community of the Ten Thousand embassies were presented to the assembly of soldiers after preliminary discussion by the generals.[3] These officials, civilian or military, could place the information against a broader background and decide how to assess its bearing and reliability.

This requirement seems to have been generally, and properly, enforced with due severity. The excited barber of the Piraeus who ran to the agora of Athens with news of the Sicilian defeat led the archons to convene a hasty assembly, at which the informant could give no clear account of how he knew. The upshot was a decision that he was a "rumor-monger" (λογοποιός) trying to upset the city, and the barber was forthwith racked on the wheel until messengers did arrive with corroborative information. The confusion in a city which could actually result from the hasty publication of ill-digested information is suggested at several points in our sources.[4]

Rumor (Φήμη) as well as true intelligence from merchants,

---

[1] Th. 1.131-32; Xen. *Hell.* 2.2, 2.4, 5.2, 6.4; Polybius 4.34.

[2] *Ath. Pol.* 43.6; Aeschines, *On the Embassy* 58. Examples appear in Th. 5.45 (Plutarch, *Alcibiades* 14.6 ff.); Xen. *Hell.* 6.4; Demosthenes 18.28, 19.17-19. In Aristophanes, *Acharnians* 61 ff., the ambassadors report to the assembly, then have dinner with the Council. G. Daverio Rocchi, *Acme* 24 (1971), p. 6, n. 3, sums up views on the relations of Council and assembly. Riepl, *Nachrichtenwesen*, pp. 430-31, discusses Greece and then takes up the role of the Senate in the Roman Republic.

[3] Xen. *Anab.* 5.6, 6.1.14.

[4] E.g., Xen. *Hell.* 5.1, 2.2; Th. 2.94; Lycurgus, *Against Leocrates* 18.

travelers, and others did nonetheless make its way into the agora
as well as into the council chambers.[1] The Greek world was an oral
world, which lacked the printed means of dissemination known in
recent centuries, and that "thronged and fragrant center", the agora,
was the place to gain the latest reports.[2] Demosthenes draws for us
an ironic picture of the Athenians running around and asking one
another, "Is there any news today?" and goes on to assail the
rumor-mongering of the market place as delusory. Philip, he
observes, may be drunk with his achievements, "but I cannot for a
moment believe that he is deliberately acting in such a way that all
the fools at Athens know what he is going to do next. For of all fools
the rumor-mongers (λογοποιοῦντες) are the worst."[3]

Eventually political intelligence—processed or raw—had almost
always to be presented to the active body of citizens or soldiers for
its information or to secure its action.[4] Sometimes publication, as
of a military result, could simply occur by announcement in the
market place; after the Hannibalic victory at Lake Trasimene the
praetor at Rome thus came into the Forum just before sunset and
proclaimed, "We are beaten in a great battle."[5] At other points a
decision by the assembly was required, so the available information
had to be laid before it to guide its decision; the standing procedure
of the Athenian assembly called for the introduction of heralds and
ambassadors as the second item of business.[6]

One of the most illuminating accounts of the deliberations which
could ensue is provided by the march of the Ten Thousand back to
the Black Sea and then to the Hellespont, under the leadership of
elected generals who governed "in obedience to the will of the major-
ity."[7] Time after time Xenophon portrays the wrangles in this
moving citizen body, where generals won not only by their own

---

[1] Aeschines, *Against Timarchus* 128 ff. (*On the Embassy* 144) and other
examples in Liddel-Scott-Jones, *Greek Lexicon* s.v. φήμη.

[2] The quotation is Pindar, fr. 91T; see for example Aristophanes, *Thesmo-
phoriazusae* 577-78, and *Plutus* 337-39; Lysias 24.19-20; R. Flacelière, *Daily
Life in Greece at the Time of Pericles* (London, 1965), pp. 147-49, sums up the
place of gossip.

[3] Demosthenes 4.10, 48-49; 19.288.

[4] Beyond earlier examples cf. Th. 4.85 ff.; Xen. *Hell.* 6.5; Plutarch, *Dion*
23.1-2, 42.4; Polyaenus 1.45.1, 1.45.4, 2.2.7.

[5] Livy 22.7.8; Polybius 3.85.7-8 indicates an assembly at the Rostra.

[6] *Ath. Pol.* 43.6; Aeschines, *Against Timarchus* 23.

[7] E.g., Xen. *Anab.* 6.1.18, 1.3, 5.6, 5.7, 6.4, 7.3.14 (vote specifically
mentioned).

force of leadership but also by their ability to assess in open speeches the immediate situation facing the army.

Once matters had been presented, especially to a regular citizen assembly, secrecy was lost, and matters were on the winds.[1] As numerous examples given in Chapter II show, enemies or other states seem always thereafter to have found out what corresponding action had been voted.[2] Still, Greek leaders whether on the march in Armenia or on the Pnyx in Athens very generally could act only with the consent of the governed as against the freedom of Philip who "did whatever he chose, without giving notice by publishing decrees, or deliberating in public."[3]

Only in a few crises can we see into the course of events in a citizen assembly, and these examples are mainly Athenian. Often the council must have presented its evaluation of political intelligence on specific matters, recommended action, and secured approval from the voters without much argument. At other times, however, matters were not so simply decided. Thus, there might be rival ambassadors to give their requests or threats, and after their reception the assembly had to choose. Before the Peloponnesian War the Spartans heard first the Corinthian envoys and then those of Athens; the Theban assembly received the ambassadors of Philip and then of Athens after Philip had begun his invasion of Boeotia.[4] Or again the meaning of the intelligence which had been reported could be interpreted variously.

Thucydides, for example, presents early in Book VI of his work speeches attributed to Nicias and Alcibiades which discuss for the Athenian assembly in some detail—but toward different conclusions—evidence of the strengths and weaknesses of the Sicilians; it has recently been suggested that Nicias, who was *proxenos* of Syracuse, may have known the island first-hand. Even more interesting are the subsequent debates in the Syracusan assembly as the first reports of the Athenian expedition arrived. The Syra-

---

[1] A politician might indeed get the assembly to act on grounds other than the real ones he had in mind. Cf. Plutarch, *Themistocles* 3-4; but note the scepticism of E. Badian, *Antichthon* 5 (1971), pp. 6 ff.; also the abortive effort reported in Plutarch, *Themistocles* 20 (*Aristides* 22). On the question of secrecy vis-a-vis the assembly Andocides, *On the Peace* 33-34, is interesting.

[2] Thus the Spartan envoys dared not make concessions concerning Pylos in the Athenian assembly; for if they did not succeed, "the terms might injure them in the opinion of their allies" (Th. 4.22).

[3] Demosthenes 18.235.

[4] Demosthenes 18.213 on the latter meeting.

cusans found it hard to believe that the Athenians really planned an attack. Hermocrates, the most far-seeing leader according to Thucydides, asserted that he was "convinced in my own mind that I have better information than anybody" and laid out the seriousness of the threat.[1] He did not reveal, at least in Thucydides' account, just what his information was even though other leaders challenged his interpretation and took the reports as rumors. In the end the Syracusan assembly at this point was persuaded only to start on initial war preparations.

In his great speech "On the Crown" Demosthenes painted in vivid, brief strokes the reaction at Athens when a messenger came in the late afternoon with news that Philip had entered Boeotia at Elatea (in 339):

> Evening had already fallen when a messenger arrived bringing to the presiding councillors [prytanes] the news that Elatea had been taken. They were sitting at supper, but they instantly rose from table ... The commotion spread through the whole city. At daybreak on the morrow the presidents summoned the Council to the Council House, and the citizens flocked to the place of assembly. Before the Council could introduce the business and prepare the agenda, the whole body of citizens had taken their places on the hill. The Council arrived, the presiding Councillors formally reported the intelligence they had received, and the courier was introduced. As soon as he had told his tale, the marshal put the question, Who wishes to speak?[2]

The news, in other words, had spread throughout the city overnight informally; when the assembly met, it heard the messenger at first hand. But who was to be able to digest this information and present a course of action? None other, naturally, than Demosthenes, who recommended first mobilization and then the despatch of an embassy to Thebes to gain its cooperation, measures which the people voted.

Let us turn from this graphic summary of the beginning of the final crisis between Philip and Athens to the earlier speeches, Philippics and Olynthiacs, in which Demosthenes had analyzed the policy of the king of Macedon for his fellow Athenians. These orations, powerful and penetrating as they are, usually concentrate on the counteraction which is demanded of Athens; and one will

---

[1] Th. 6.33; on Nicias, see Green, *Armada from Athens*, pp. 4-5.
[2] Demosthenes 18.169-70.

search in vain for any specific bits of intelligence to support the orator's concept of the Macedonian ruler. Demosthenes will say no more than "I have heard" or "I know from one who had lived there, incapable of falsehood."[1] A modern reader really learns more from this corpus of speeches about the means by which Philip could find out Athenian views, including actors and local Quislings.[2]

Yet these orations, together with earlier examples, are significant testimony in their very omissions. Citizens in the Greek *poleis* were evidently not to be swayed primarily by specific assessments of political intelligence. Far more important would have been their belief that a leader *did* have better information or at least had adequate information for the course he proposed. They accepted him as a man of foresight and sound counsel—

> the man who from first to last had closely watched the sequence of events, and had rightly fathomed the purposes and the desires of Philip; for anyone who had not grasped those purposes, or had not studied them long beforehand... was not the man to appreciate the needs of the hour, or to find any counsel to offer to the people.[3]

Is this situation really very different in modern states?

Political leaders like Hermocrates probably had no special command of specific reports,[4] but they had acquired over the years a great store of general information about other states, the way they had acted in previous events, and the character of their leaders. Thus the Corinthians could seek to upset the aged stereotype, which they asserted the Spartans held, by their own more recent experience. Demosthenes repeatedly summarized recent actions of Philip to suggest what he would do next, or informed his fellow citizens how war in their day differed from that of earlier times.[5]

---

[1] Demosthenes 1.22, 2.17, 8.14; in 2.3 he asserts that he could give the resources (ῥώμην) of Philip. Aeschines, *Against Ctesiphon* 77, incidentally explains how Demosthenes received the news of the death of Philip later (by spies of an Athenian general) but pretended he had the information by a dream (Plutarch, *Demosthenes* 22). One might contrast the approach of Pres. J. F. Kennedy, during the Cuban missile crisis of 1962, who presented aerial photographs and naval reports to support the argument of his television speeches.

[2] Demosthenes 4.18, 5.6, 7.23.

[3] Demosthenes 18.172.

[4] Hermocrates does assert that the most prominent Athenian general was opposed to the expedition (Th. 6.34). Did he know this, or is the remark a foreshadowing by Thucydides?

[5] Demosthenes 9.48-52, 18.18 ff., etc.

By the late fifth and fourth centuries history had come to be a conscious literary discipline in Greece, and its information could have practical utility. Andocides began his defense of the negotiations with Sparta by asserting, "one must use the past as a guide to the future," though we must not picture a tyranny of the past over the present. Even Demosthenes, who so often cited earlier events, observed, "No one proposes deliberation about the past; it is the present and the future that call the statesman to his post."[1]

Against this background of general information those who possessed it most fully could interpret a specific piece of intelligence. Such persons would not be the ordinary citizens of the assembly who "display an interest only so long as you sit here listening, or when some fresh item of news arrives; after that, each man goes home, and not only pays no attention to public business, but does not even recall it to mind."[2] Rather, it was men like Themistocles, Pericles, Demosthenes, the elders who had sat in the Council, and more generally across Greece the aristocrats who held in their minds the information which made intelligence useful.

The words "in their minds" require stress. It would be difficult to assess how much written intelligence material any Greek state had on hand; but most information was preserved and passed on primarily in an oral form. Demosthenes put this fact in succinct form, "the political system is based upon speeches."[3] Ambassadors were commonly sent out in groups; the speech of Aeschines *On the Embassy* in 343 B.C. gives a vivid picture of their individual and oral reports to the assembly concerning the course of negotiations with

---

[1] Andocides, *On the Peace* 2; Demosthenes 18.192. Cf. my *Awakening of the Greek Historical Spirit*, pp. 147 ff. In Demosthenes 6.10 ff. Philip "draws a lesson from the past;" Aeschines, *On the Embassy* 28 ff. appeals to history. Other aspects of this awareness of a relation of past and present are Plutarch, *Timoleon* 11.4; the argument from the Cypselid tyranny in Hdt. 5.92; or, to take just one play by Aristophanes, the references in *Lysistrata* to Hippias, Cleomenes, Aristogeiton, Artemisia, Artemisium, etc.

[2] Demosthenes 10.1. Such a comment does not entirely agree with the spirit of Th. 2.40; but the remarks attributed to Cleon in Th. 3.38 are not inconsistent with it. Wilensky, *Organizational Intelligence*, pp. 148-49, comments on the fact that modern media of communication concentrate on crises as against "the routine truth."

[3] Demosthenes 19.184, a noble statement; but anyone who has sought to disentangle the truth about the relative roles of Aeschines and Demosthenes in Athenian foreign policy (with relation especially to Philip), as presented in their conflicting speeches, must sympathize with the Athenian assembly and juries which had to distinguish true from false.

Philip—though not one which fully coincides with the rebuttal later delivered by Demosthenes.

As far as written information is concerned, we could not expect to find detailed intelligence reports and assessments of the modern type or even the analyses of the character of foreign armies—and the way to deal with each—which were composed in Byzantine times.[1] Information about other states was available to Greek statesmen and orators, to judge from references, primarily in the form of the histories of Herodotus and Thucydides or in the geographical framework of Xenophon's *Anabasis*. Even here, however, it is worth noting that the picture of Athenian history in Aeschines' *On the Embassy* was essentially a repetition of the error-filled account which the orator Andocides had delivered almost fifty years earlier.[2]

Archival reports which might in any sense be considered under the heading of intelligence were limited, as far as references in the sources are concerned, to resolutions, decrees, and summaries of the personnel and dates of embassies despatched abroad (or sometimes those received from other states). Before meeting an embassy Antigonus the One-Eyed "used previously to inform himself from the public records, who were the persons that composed the last embassy from the same quarter, the subject of it, and every particular relative to it."[3]

---

[1] To give a published example (in the *Atlantic Monthly*, July 1972, pp. 36-49) George W. Ball, Undersecretary of State, composed a long memorandum against American policy in South Vietnam in 1964. This document cites cables, intelligence estimates, planning papers, speeches by Vietnamese leaders and American officials, discussions with European counterparts, and the experience of the earlier involvement in Korea as reported by historians and newspaper opinions to support Ball's argument. For Byzantine discussions of foreign ways of fighting see K. Krumbacher, *Geschichte der byzantinischen Literatur* (Munich, 1897), p. 258.

[2] Aeschines, *On the Embassy* 172 ff. = Andocides, *On the Peace* 3 ff. The Loeb editor of Aeschines (C. D. Adams) cites the acid criticism of this account by Eduard Meyer, *Forschungen zur Alten Geschichte*, II (Halle, 1899), pp. 132 ff.

[3] Polyaenus 4.6.2 (though one must wonder in the case of this marshal of Alexander which public records could be meant). Aeschines, *On the Embassy* 58, attests that the dates and names of ambassadors were carefully listed; in the same speech (32) resolutions and names of voters on resolutions of a congress of Greek states are cited. On archives see now Ernst Posner, *Archives in the Ancient World* (Cambridge, Mass., 1972), pp. 91-117.

CHAPTER FIVE

LIMITS AND MISUSE OF INTELLIGENCE

Whenever a historian studies a set of ancient problems in the light of modern conditions, he must keep clearly in mind the ancient context of those problems. It may, indeed, be useful to cite parallels of our own day; and at several points in the foregoing discussion the complexity of contemporary intelligence needs has been particularly stressed. If a modern state is not to be surprised technologically, its experts must watch the most hidden and theoretical developments in the sciences elsewhere; to gauge one's own requirements in intercontinental weapons and other devices requires a thorough, sound knowledge of the armaments of potential enemies, even though this panoply is ever changing.

Such references, however, must not be taken as inferring that classic Greece would have shared these concerns for political intelligence in the same degree or sought to cope with them in the same ways. The evidence advanced in previous chapters may suffice to demonstrate that there *was* an interest in knowing the capabilities and plans of other states, and the fact that the historian must ferret out very scattered, almost accidental references to the methods of gathering information does not, in itself, prove that they were not rather commonly practised. In many problems which may interest modern scholars the ancient sources are equally tantalizing in their spasmodic illumination simply because their authors did not happen to have our interests. If the ancient historians in particular often do not bother to give specific information as to how a fact had been learned, we must remember first that the footnote did not yet exercise its tyranny over the historical mind and, secondly, that even in modern studies of general scope, comparable to the major Greek histories, the reader is not often given this information.

Nonetheless there were inherent limits in the Greek world both in the search for intelligence and for its utilization. As Wilensky notes, "the more an organization sees its external environment and internal relations as rationalized ... the more resources it will devote to the intelligence function."[1] Such a rationalization of political life was

---

[1] Wilensky, *Organizational Intelligence*, p. 14; cf. his remarks on the relations between complexity of structure and the need for experts (pp. 38-39).

only partially operative in ancient Greece, and in consequence the modes of gaining information could be often very simple, almost automatic.

Again, the Greek world was a relatively static structure. Most of its inhabitants were subsistence farmers; technology changed slowly, if at all; the political patterns of the *polis*, once set, did not alter greatly. Military operations were slow and predictable to a degree which often surprises modern students, in the manner of the eighteenth century when it was common to have armies "stand at bay within view of one another, and spend a whole campaign in dodging, or as it is genteelly called, observing one another, and then march off into winter quarters."[1] The leaders and generals of one state might calculate the strengths of opponents on very limited specific data and could evaluate enemy plans largely in terms of their own methods of operation.

Polybius' assertion that Greek states in early times did not seek the advantages of secrecy and treachery does not entirely reflect the reality of interstate relations; yet it is true that secrecy was not likely to extend beyond the tactical level of a sudden raid or spoiling attack.[2] Pericles even boasts in his Funeral Oration that "our city is thrown open to the world, and we never expel a foreigner or prevent him from seeing or learning anything of which the secret if revealed to an enemy might profit him."[3] Essentially this openness may have been characteristic of many Greek states, though Athenian dockyards probably were not entirely available for public inspection. The Spartan government, however, did not operate in quite such a limelight. During the Plataean campaign it kept the Athenian envoys dancing in anxious doubt whether its army would march, and informed them only after the troops had actually left; at one point in the Peloponnesian War Thucydides remarks that he cannot tell the strength of the Lacedaemonian army at Mantinea because of "the secrecy of the government."[4]

---

[1] Daniel Defoe, quoted by Nef, *War and Human Progress*, p. 156. Note the observation of Marshall Saxe, quoted by Hoffman Nickerson, *The Armed Horde* (New York, 1942), p. 53, after Foch, "I do not favor battles, especially at the beginning of a war. I am sure that a clever general can wage it as long as he lives without being compelled to battle." Compare the criticism of Greek warfare by Mardonius in Hdt. 7.9.

[2] E.g., Hdt. 5.74, 6.132; Th. 1.101, 5.54, 5.56.

[3] Th. 2.39.

[4] Hdt. 9.11; Th. 5.68.

A more serious limitation on political intelligence than any efforts at secrecy probably was the very fact that even the leaders of any one state had a rather limited amount of statistical data or precise information on their own community. Pericles could lay before the Athenian assembly a reckoning of its troops, ships, and reserves of money,[1] and a century later Demosthenes made somewhat elaborate calculations (or guesses) about the wealth of the Athenian citizenry in proposing reforms of the trierarchy.[2] Most states must have had some elementary form of census, partly for financial reasons but also to determine which citizens were of age to serve in war;[3] thereby they might calculate whether they could act in a specific difficulty.[4] But precise figures scarcely went further, and even these were not beyond some doubt in view of ancient limits on reckoning.[5]

Although serious limitations were inherent in the possibilities of gathering political intelligence, the techniques of acquiring and assessing information must have been essentially adequate in the Greek world. Modern historians perhaps assume too readily that each state was completely aware of the intentions which were being

---

[1] Th. 2.13; cf. the jest of Alcibiades in Plutarch, *Alcibiades* 7.2. That such information could then enter into public memory is shown by Xen. *Anab.* 7.1.27; Andocides, *On the Peace* 7 ff.; and Aeschines, *On the Embassy* 172 ff.

[2] E.g., Demosthenes 3.24, 3.28, 4.13 ff., 20.32, 20.77.

[3] In Plutarch, *Nicias* 14.5, the Athenians are said to have captured a Syracusan ship with tablets on which were lists of citizens by tribes for military purposes; the report itself may be doubted in view of his own remark that other scholars dated this event to a much later occasion. Th. 6.17, 6.20-23 gives information on the numbers in Sicily; Hdt. 4.81, the curious devices for numbering inhabitants in Scythia. For the census at Athens and deme registers (ληξιαρχικὰ γραμματεῖα) we know far less than one might wish. Cf. PW s.v. Δῆμοι, col. 27 (v. Schoeffer); the "Themistocles decree," lines 29-30 (M. H. Jameson, *Hesperia* 29 [1960], pp. 198 ff.); Plutarch, *Pericles* 37; Aeschines, *Against Timarchus* 77. A casual reference by Lysias 16.6 shows that the Athenian cavalry lists at least were not entirely accurate.

[4] In Xen. *Hell.* 6.1 the Spartans calculated on the base of information given by Polydamas and decided that they could not stop Jason; note the comparative figures in Demosthenes 4.20 ff.

[5] Cf. G. D. Mickwitz, "Economic Rationalism in Graeco-Roman Agriculture", *English Historical Review* 208 (1937), pp. 577-89, with whom G. E. M. de Ste Croix, "Greek and Roman Accounting," *Studies in the History of Accounting* (London, 1956), pp. 14-74, agrees. One may doubt that ancient Greeks deliberately opposed censuses lest "an annual register of our people, will acquaint our enemies abroad with our weakness, and a return of the poor's rate, our enemies at home with our wealth" (Mr. Thornton, MP York, in a debate on an English register in 1753, Hansard, *Parliamentary Debates*, 14 [London, 1813], p. 1319 under 26 George II).

developed within the political structures of its opponents; in ancient Greece as in the modern world the intelligence available to a *polis* must often have been incomplete or even erroneous.[1] Yet major disasters as a result of faulty intelligence were not common in the classical period, though local surprises might occur.

This is not to say that intelligence was always properly used. Leaders could make mistakes; far more serious were faulty decisions by the body of citizens as a whole. "How shall the people if it cannot form true judgments, be able rightly to direct the state?"

The most famous exemple in this respect is the disastrous Athenian expedition to Syracuse, 415-13 B.C. As a modern observer, however, reads the accounts in Thucydides and Plutarch's lives of Nicias and Alcibiades, he can scarcely conclude that this disaster resulted from a lack of intelligence per se. Few operations were launched in ancient Greece with greater forethought and care in preparation; the expedition is probably the best ancient proof of Wilensky's comment that "Ironically, a 'hasty' decision made under pressure may on average be better than a less urgent one."[2]

Thucydides does begin his account with the observation that most Athenians knew nothing of the great size of Sicily and of its numerous population, but in the debates which preceded the launching of the attack Nicias drew an ample picture of the problems involved, and the citizens accepted his figures of the great strength which would be required for the expedition.[3] Plutarch even gives the piquant detail that young and old alike drew maps of Sicily and the relative position of Libya and Carthage.[4] Later, during the dreary course of the operations in Sicily, Nicias was extremely careful in the despatches home to present a full picture; and even went so far as to write out his remarks lest his messengers fail to inform the assembly properly.[5]

---

[1] An interesting recent exploration of the defects of intelligence, and the alterations in Argive policies which accompanied change in information, is given by Thomas Kelly with regard to the destruction of Panactum, in *Historia* 21 (1972), pp. 159-69. Other illustrations could be developed by more detailed analysis of the course of interstate relations than is warranted here; the historian looking back on an event is often more omniscient than the participants.

[2] The preceding quotation is from Euripides, *Suppliants* 417-18; the later, from Wilensky, *Organizational Intelligence*, p. 76.

[3] Th. 6.9 ff.

[4] Plutarch, *Nicias* 12.1 and *Alcibiades* 17.3.

[5] Th. 7.8, 7.11-15; Plutarch, *Nicias* 19.7.

In a general evaluation of the course of the Peloponnesian War after the death of Pericles, the historian Thucydides calls the Sicilian expedition the greatest error, "not that the Athenians miscalculated their enemy's power, but they themselves, instead of consulting for the interests of the expedition which they had sent out, were occupied in intriguing against one another for the leadership of the democracy."[1] To this contention we might add the blunders and overconfidence of the citizen body itself, and its reluctance to reverse itself as conditions changed—democratic characteristics not unknown at various points in World Wars I and II.[2] The Syracusans, on the other side, failed to react rapidly to news of the Athenian expedition, not because they lacked information but because they feared the creation of internal tyrants if they concentrated their strength and leadership.

The major fault in the use of intelligence within the Greek world lay in the degree to which the citizenry of a state could evaluate and act rationally on the information presented to it. One problem, which can be illustrated in the Athenian reaction to Philip's aggression, was the slowness with which the Athenian assembly took steps and its unwillingness to embark on a positive program against quiet subversion. Too often the fellow-citizens of Andocides shared his view, "Peace means safety and power for the democracy, whereas war means its downfall."[3] When Demosthenes told his compatriots that Philip gobbled up states without formal declaration of war and they did nothing, a modern student will think of the reluctance of French and English citizen bodies to counter Hitler's steps from the occupation of the Rhineland on to the days of Munich. To quote Andocides again, many Athenians felt that nothing could ever be settled by the assembly. "No one, they argue, has ever yet saved the Athenian people by open persuasion; measures for its good must be secret or disguised."[4]

Another difficulty was the popular tendency to think in terms of

---

[1] Th. 2.65.

[2] Wilensky, *Organizational Intelligence*, pp. 78-79: "When confronted with undeniable disconfirmation men do not merely defend their convictions; under some conditions—when their belief is strong, when they have committed themselves with some important act which is difficult to disavow, and when they have social support in their denial of reality—they do so with reborn fervor".

[3] Andocides, *On the Peace* 12; repeated by Aeschines, *On the Embassy* 177. Note Demosthenes' scorn of this line of argument in 19.88, 99.

[4] Andocides, *On the Peace* 33.

stereotypes, a factor again not unknown in modern times in which concepts of perfidious Albion, Teutonic savagery, and so on "can for years remain impervious to evidence."[1] In tragedy and comedy alike the Athenians received reenforcement for simplicistic views of Thebes and Sparta;[2] early in the present work mention was made of the Spartan stereotype of Athens which the Corinthians felt they had to destroy if they were to secure Spartan help.

Is this latter picture, however, anything more than a sophistic device which Thucydides employed to introduce the main thrust of the Corinthian argument? Did the Spartans in 432 still hold that picture of a self-sacrificing Athens which they *might* have established in the days of Marathon and Salamis? In the speech by king Archidamus, part of which was quoted in Chapter I, the Spartans do not appear to have been ignorant of Athenian financial and naval resources; more generally, it may be doubted that the Spartans really were less able than the Athenians in gathering and making use of intelligence.

There is, to be sure, the comment of Euripides in his *Suppliants* that "states, whose policy is dark and cautious, have their sight darkened by their carefulness."[3] Yet when Aristagoras of Miletus sought aid against the Persians first from the Spartans and then from the Athenians, he failed utterly to persuade the Spartan king Cleomenes but before the Athenian assembly won support by his arguments of the riches available in Asia and the inefficiency of the Persian army; Herodotus observes thereon, "It seems indeed to be easier to deceive a multitude than one man."[4]

The kings and ephors of Sparta might be slow of speech and content to abide within their native valley, but across the course of Greek history down at least to 404 they seem to have been able to

---

[1] Wilensky, *Organizational Intelligence*, p. 40.

[2] E.g., Euripides, *Suppliants* 187; *Andromache* passim (on the assertion in lines 451-52 that the Spartans say one thing and mean another cf. Th. 5.105, Hdt. 9.54). For that matter one can also find the stereotype that Athens interferes in other states; compare Th. 1.70 and Euripides, *Suppliants* 576-77. See also Martin, *La Vie internationale*, p. 70. In using the word "reenforcement" in the text I intend to suggest that comic and tragic poets certainly did not originate information but rather reflected it, as in Aristophanes, *Acharnians* 514 ff. and *Peace* 605 ff. on the causes of the Peloponnesian War.

[3] Euripides, *Suppliants* 324-25.

[4] Hdt. 5.97; cf. Euripides, *Suppliants* 410 ff.

sense the problems of the Greek world. Note, for example, their constant stress on the liberation of the Greeks from Athenian enslavement as a leitmotif in their propaganda and actions in the Peloponnesian War itself.

Thereafter, in the years from 404 to 371, the Spartans lost the mastery they had achieved in the Aegean world. Generally this collapse is attributed to "a new range of demands of all sorts suddenly imposed on men and on a system too uncivilised to cope with them," which brought in the end those evidences of internal decay stressed by Aristotle.[1] The root of the matter, however, was the Spartan decision, taken only in doubt and executed in wavering fashion, to maintain open power over *poleis* whose essential character forced them always to seek independence. This decision led the Spartans into a hopeless, long protracted struggle and may in a sense be accounted a failure to appreciate the fundamental character of the Greek state system.[2] Yet one must give the Spartans the credit for meditating on the fact that they had had to protect Greece first from the Persians and then from Athenian imperialism in a truly terrible struggle, and deciding that their earlier withdrawals had been an error.

Undoubtedly the Spartans made local mistakes during the period 404-371 in judging the particular conditions in a *polis*, as in their seizure of Thebes; but at least one event deserves better note. The speed, that is, with which the Spartans acted on getting reports about Persian naval preparations, as brought by Herodas, is an impressive illustration of their ability to integrate a vital bit of news with a general background of information.[3] Of this particular skill there is, indeed, scarcely a better example in all Greek history.

It is difficult to compare fully the ability of the two greatest states in Greece to assess and act on intelligence by reason of the relative lack of information from within Sparta itself. Intuitively perhaps one may yet conclude that the asserted slow-wittedness of the one side was at least matched by the handicaps of the Athenian

---

[1] W. G. Forrest, *A History of Sparta, 950-192 B.C.* (Norton paperback, 1969), p. 125. Ste Croix, *Origins of the Peloponnesian War*, pp. 151 ff., judges Spartan foreign policy rather more harshly than would I.

[2] It could, however, perhaps be said that the Athenians failed even more obviously to understand this; for the Second Athenian Confederacy was shattered by reason of Athenian conduct in the fourth century which had learned nothing from the disaster of the fifth century.

[3] See above, p. 23.

assembly on the other—not so much its proverbial fickleness but rather the terrific difficulties an orator encountered in shaking the stereotypes and inherent slowness of fundamental change in a self-satisfied multitude of voters.[1]

The Greek *poleis* faced their worst problems in dealing with states outside the ordinary Hellenic pattern of political organization. In the classical period Persia was the most important political power of a different type. Persia and the Greeks, in dealing with each other, were occasionally mutually baffled by the customs of the other side or by its aims. The negotiations between Sparta and the satrap Tissaphernes which led to Persian support for the Spartan navy in the closing stages of the Peloponnesian War were thus bedevilled by the Great King's insistence on reclaiming all the Greeks he had ever ruled, and by Tissaphernes' suspicions of the meaning of the Spartan propaganda for "freedom."[2] Although Alcibiades was so successful in seeing into the satrap's mind that he could manipulate Tissaphernes to his own ends, the Spartans seem to have floundered badly, whereas Tissaphernes appears in the end to have been able to assess Spartan needs and motives.[3] In urging aid for the Rhodians, Demosthenes feels that he can predict the actions of Artemisia of Caria but "as to the King, I should not like to say that I know what he is actually going to do."[4]

As is so often the case in considering the relations of Greeks and Persians, the historian is handicapped here by a lack of independent information from the Persian side. Somehow the Persian central administration did gain a basic background of intelligence by which it could decide what steps to take in the ever-shifting political relations among the Greek states. More than once it intervened to help reduce the power of a temporary victor;[5] it seems to have been at least partly aware of the growing threat from Macedon. Generally, again, the Persian king and his court appear to have been able to

---

[1] Wilensky, *Organizational Intelligence*, pp. 118-19, presents an inconclusive discussion as to whether a democracy is better in getting and using intelligence than a totalitarian state.

[2] Th. 8.5, 8.37, 8.43, 8.52, 8.58; on Persian suspicion of *eleutheria*, Th. 8.46, 8.52. Tissaphernes does not appear to have spoken Greek himself (Th. 8.45, 8.56, 8.85; Xen. *Anab.* 2.3.17).

[3] Th. 8.78, 8.83, 8.87; Plutarch, *Alcibiades* 24.

[4] Demosthenes 15.12-13.

[5] Polyaenus 7.16.2 asserts that this was Artaxerxes' deliberate policy (cf. earlier Xen. *Hell.* 1.5).

assess the information provided to them by exiles from the time of Hippias and Demaratus on through Conon and others in the fourth century.[1]

Once the Athenians captured a Persian envoy at Eion, on his way to Sparta during the Peloponnesian War, and read his despatches (written in cuneiform); the main point was a complaint that the king "could not understand what they [the Spartans] wanted; for, although many envoys had come to him, no two of them agreed."[2] Especially in the fourth century, when embassies from Thebes, Athens, Sparta, and other states were constantly on the road to the Great King, this problem must have been compounded manyfold. On the other hand news of the simple life of Agesilaus or of the victory of Leuctra is said to have spread into the interior of Asia,[3] and Demosthenes assumed that naturally information from his native agora was reported to the King.[4]

We can only speculate that reports from the Ionian and Phrygian satraps, together with the trips of Persian envoys and agents themselves,[5] did provide a body of information. Persian archives may have built up information in a more conscious manner than in most Greek states, or at the least contact between Persia and the Greeks was sufficiently intense to keep intelligence in the active memory of the King's advisers. During the long course of Greco-Persian relations down to the time of Alexander, the two sides did manage to acquire enough information about each other's practices and aims to be able to co-exist.[6]

The same cannot be said of Rome and Greece in the dismal days

---

[1] Cf. the value set on Themistocles' advice in Plutarch, *Themistocles* 29; the advice by Conon to Pharnabazus in Xen. *Hell.* 4.8.

[2] Th. 4.50. Interrogation of Spartan ambassadors as to conditions in Greece is indicated also in Aristophanes, *Acharnians* 647 ff.

[3] Plutarch, *Agesilaus* 14.1 and *Pelopidas* 30.2-3.

[4] Demosthenes 10.32, 14.28, 14.38.

[5] E.g., the expedition of Democedes in Hdt. 3.134-36; or the efforts at bribery reported for the fifth century by Th. 1.109 (cf. p. 21, n. 3 above) and for the fourth by Xen. *Hell.* 3.5 and *Hell. Oxy.* 2.2, 13.1 (see I. A. F. Bruce, *An Historical Commentary on the 'Hellenica Oxyrhynchia'* [Cambridge, 1967], pp. 58-60). Alexander is reported to have found letters from Demosthenes at Sardis (Plutarch, *Demosthenes* 20.5). See generally Posner, *Archives*, pp. 118-27.

[6] Note however the view Aeschines takes of a letter from the Persian king, which he considers insolent and barbarous (*Against Ctesiphon* 238). I hope to explore more fully elsewhere the relations of Greeks and Persians, a subject on which conventional views do not appear entirely justified.

from the Second Macedonian War onwards. The events of the second century B.C. reflect the most terrible failure of Greek intelligence procedures as "the clouds that loom in the west" settled down on Hellas.[1] The Greeks could not comprehend that entirely different world in which concepts such as *fides, deditio, amicus populi Romani* had each a special significance; nor, on the Roman side, were the generals and senators of the Republic able to grasp the sophisticated, shifting character of Greek politics.[2]

This comment, true, is a sweeping statement which would require a great deal of qualification were we to consider Greek history after 336 in detail; for one thing, individual Roman leaders did from time to time show an ability to divide or win over Greek elements, both states and also internal factions. Nonetheless, the meeting of Romans and Greeks, operating within systems of very different principles, suggests that in such a situation the usual patterns of gathering and assessing information must fail. The Greek world would in any case have fallen before the might of Roman arms, divided and weakened as the major components of Hellas were, but mutual incomprehension helped to make the saddening series of explosions the more inevitable and more devastating in their consequences.

---

[1] Polybius 5.104.10 (217 B.C.). R. M. Errington, *The Dawn of Empire* (Ithaca, N.Y., 1972), pp. 107 ff., considers Demetrius of Pharos the first "to misunderstand the nature of his free relationship with Rome."

[2] On the complicated history of the second century B.C. see recently E. Badian, *Foreign Clientelae (264-70 B.C.)* (Oxford, 1958), pp. 55 ff.; John Briscoe, "Rome and The Class Struggle in the Greek States 200-140 B.C.," *Past and Present* 36 (1967), pp. 3-20; J. Deininger, *Der politische Widerstand gegen Rom in Griechenland 217 bis 86 v. Chr.* (Berlin, 1971); E. Will, *Histoire politique du monde hellénistique, 323-30 av. J.-C.*, II (Nancy, 1967), pp. 126 ff. An interesting example of the parallel difficulty of American generals in understanding the complicated patterns of European state rivalries, which probably will not be known to many readers, is afforded by the documents in vol. 10 of *United States Army in the World War, 1917-1919* (Washington, 1948), which express surprise, irritation, and horror at the intermixture of political and military action by the Allies after the Armistice.